AIMLESS LIFE

by the same author

The Poet in the Poem
W. H. Auden
Shakespeare's Metrical Art

AIMLESS LIFE: POEMS: 1961-1995

George T. Wright

North Stone Editions
Minneapolis, Minnesota

1999

First published in 1999
by North Stone Editions Limited
Box 14098
Minneapolis, Minnesota
55414-0098

First Edition

Manufactured in the United States of America

North Stone Editions are published for James Naiden
by North Stone Limited
Box 14098, Minneapolis, Minnesota 55414-0098
United States of America

This book is printed in an edition of 1500 copies softbound, 250 cloth.

For my wife Jerry

Forty Years Together

all this time our
tangle, our
composition, our
fathomless regard

ACKNOWLEDGMENTS

Acknowledgments are made to the editors of the following magazines or books in which some of these poems first appeared: *A Coloring Book for Adults, ADE Bulletin, Arizona Quarterly, Carolina Quarterly, Centennial Review, Counter/Measures, Dacotah Territory, Druid, Esquire, Gramercy Review, The Nation, (New) American Review, The North Stone Review, Outcast, Poetry Northwest, Sewanee Review, Southern Quarterly*, and *Tennessee Poetry Journal.*

"Aquarium" originally appeared in *The New Yorker* and *The New Yorker Book of Poems.*

TABLE OF CONTENTS

Roots and Epitaphs

Academic Affairs

Classical Failings

Jiggling the Mirror

Prologue: LATE LETTER TO MY FATHER

I

Young man, you had
trouble, those epic days,
finding yourself, faring
from venture to venture, verging
on success, on failure.

I know that road, I wove
my own wanderer years, and so
did my brother, before we
tracked our tallest selves
through to flatland and clearing

and became natives: purveyors,
for wary transients,
of square meals or poems.
Then here for a while, we supposed,
we fit, we belong here.

When in world squalls
your own craft foundered,
you were lucky enough to be
bailed out by an elder
bachelor brother –

to which you responded,
through years that crested your strength,
with the grave ties, straight back, timely
haircuts, stock opinions
of a New York Saxon.

In later life I surprise you
in our uptown apartment's
foyer, poised and pained,
but whether arriving or leaving
I can't make out.

Gentle, evasive,
like some of your progeny,
skillful at games of chance,
not greatly gifted
but shrewdly adapted,

restless, you would
get up nights to pace
and cough up your war,
your one souvenir
of no-man's land.

II

As I grow older,
I have adopted you,
scar-weary, minder of forms,
your headaches, your habit
of going quiet at stress.

You learned to hate Caesar
at my own high school
(roots of a sort there).
By far the surer scholar,
I have come no further.

A dark manse down the street
housed *your* growing up.
When we moved away,
what wrench did it cost you
to strike that childhood,

setting in train the motions
that in *my* life have thrown me
westward and elsewhere,
your other children
equally scattered,

drifters, as little directed
as Huns or Vandals,
seizing the chances
that offered, anywhere away from
centers of pressure?

We tramp around the globe
as it gets hotter.
If we believed in purposes,
it was your part,
sage prince of barbarians,

to take us this far down
the road out, or back,
traditional looters,
feeders at Frankish troughs
or farms in Vermont

but never in place for more than
one, two generations,
our honor to be,
among others rooted and violent,
at heart homeless.

III

I have to think for a moment
where you're buried.
When you died, like a good Goth I
was off on a trip, and in fifteen
years I've not seen your grave.

Now that I work it through,
this way we have
of abandoning every position
without strict loss
to keep some central composure,

this weakness for chronic exile
disguised as settling,
is shared more widely than we think:
not wholly shameful,
not continually rankling,

but a foraging outward to find
what abides in crisis.
When in my turn I became
a temporary soldier,
I remember, I cherish

your touch and concern:
the Pict or Viking son
weaving across the waters
to pick up a war,
your own modernized,

yourself re-armored,
with all those forebears,
to kill one another again
on the same bloody battlefield,
the twenty-year reunion

of ancient brawlers.
Over-age, envious, younger
than I am now,
you drove me through our city
at four in the morning,

gripped goodbye at the bus station.
No more poignant image
of love and war,
of our common drift,
has blessed my aimless life.

Private Plot

New Locale (Knoxville)

SUMMER VOICES

I

"Who was it on the phone?" I have to think,
Head rising from a pool of books and ink:
"A wrong number." But I let go the tight
Muscle of ideas, turn out the light.
Lord! the green summer sponges the still room,
The evening yells of kids resound, resume.
A million nails, thoughts, volts ago *I* get
To yell like that. The wish is in me yet.
So is the act, but faint: when I rejoice
Now, I am grown-up, have a basser voice,
Command my neighbors with my yearly pay,
Open my door and shoo the poor away.
Beyond my window waits my screaming car:
We have no need to yell out what we are.

II

"I'm going next door." Indoor shouts don't count,
Only the kind that question the air and mount
(So my ear claims) to some more golden region,
Given to evening baseball and religion,
Where voices clap like baseballs in the glove,
And sounds can seem the deepest form of love,
Edging to music, singing in a choir,
Before three candles or around a fire,
Some faithful reed a third below the rest,
Laughed at but loved, where any noise is blessed –
Rhythms and holds that happen to me still
When I watch dusk occur or climb a hill
And come into that thrilled maternal calm
In which whatever is tells how I am.

III

"Ted, guess what happened?" That is all I guess,
Articulate on most degrees of mess.
A child is ill, a car has killed a cat,
Neighbors are selling, Ruth dropped in to chat.
Though every breath is still astonishing,
I sometimes think there's no new *kind* of thing.
Spring's never obvious, never a bore,
But all its general has been said before.
Only the particular is new,
And therefore as I age I change my view,
Attend to leaves and snowflakes, seek event
In patterned rest or patterned argument,
And concentrate on sounds that steer me back
To some first moment from the yackety-yak.

IV

"We ought to talk." And yet today is real –
Flows, flames beneath the fantasies I feel,
It insists, it is willful, it requires,
It thumps and jangles, it evokes and tires.
A local structure, gaping, condemned, I shall,
I must, keep building in this new locale,
Once gorgeous, lately a bit shot, bowering still
Old grace, rare warmth even as it puffs downhill.
These shouts I hear come from outside my mind;
The life that leads me's not yet all defined.
Dog is this dog and barks, love is this night
Riding its joint past to an edge of light.
The neighbor lepers in me rise and walk.
Even when all is said, we ought to talk.

IMPROMPTUS

1. Inner City

On a summer evening like any other,
children's cries lobbed from their distant play,
machines at hum in far yards (motorbikes, mowers),
the sky about to withdraw modestly, and the houselight
beginning to clean the unshouted streets.
Inside, only a fly's buzz nerves the silence.

Can the day end with such aplomb while I
quake and heave in hurt and anger?

2. Inside during a Storm

Rummaging in the Romantics, I turn to the sudden storm.
Branches wave and lunge, rain pours on the lawn,
groaning thunder shakes the whole world I stand in,
and in this dark of day lightning tears the dirty cloth.

It ought to be sublime; the jet caught in these clouds
is small as it scoots by. *What force! Vastness! Look, Byron!*
But I notice my window is streaked, and I turn again to the book
where Wordsworth says it's the feeling must make the event matter.

3. Intimation

I see a sudden pool beside my desk,
a bay in my book. There I am idle
and in sun brown, young
                              . . . it's gone now,
I sit at my work, the papers don't even blow
against me, merely weigh.

Give me rest, O things as they are.

DEPOSIT

for my brother

I

It's a long time now since I
paddled a canoe in the moonlight,

myself a boy on the Manasquan,
weaving slowly, weaving among the crabnets,

their poles slanting, the netting delicate in the dark.
Above, stirring the air, pools of gnats,

and lights from farther cottages
marking the edges of the shallow water.

II

Years later, holding an oar over the water,
trying to hear whether anything still stands still,

I peer, only survivor, into the ripples
cast by the oar that drips into the dark water.

Of air, I pause on this side of the border,
but still am moved to see how, keeping quiet,

aslant, astir,
that unvexed river has its hours of flood.

BEYOND WINTER

To find a form of words for the falling snow,
the bare tips of trees and the gray air,
and for the life of me who see what is near
as large, what's immediate as mine and general:
the dog lapping water, and the sleep
rising and falling in the room above,
beneath the snow, within the saving house,
or silent in the center of my waking.

Nothing comes back in the human root.
The fall wind only furthers, not clears the board.
Spring is ironic as it rubs us young.
Some pulse goes on counting, and the score will scrape.
Around the days simply to be here is best,
to wake from sleep, and to let sleep, let sleep,
keep track of the faint acquisitions of trees, and find
resisting word-forms for the large drifting snow.

SPRING

Spring shows an ankle, I fall on my face
As this year's wish forgets what green is like.
Now the fruit trees start spraying their white grace,
My cheeks are young again, and I could make
Love to the goddess of all this, but ache
       With consciousness of Time, that boils my egg,
       Colors the leaf and sprays pain through my leg.

O pulse that never trips, what of that girl
Who in the local way is got up wrong
But lives her walk, constraint within a whirl,
Casual purpose like a voiceless song
Edging her step, making her meaning long,
       As she flares by me through the lot of cars,
       Deliberately, to stir up waves and wars.

How I should like (O vain, deluded wretch!)
In her surprised, not too remorseful bed,
To be a boy at absolute hard stretch,
Driving away the dragon Maidenhead!
But age, alas, as divers wits have said,
       Decrees us different apogees, and Time,
       That gave me verdure once, now leaves me rime.

Four butterflies askew across the yard
Fly through my moment into my poem and
Are swallowed by existence like a sword.
To keep the springtime steady to my hand,
I need a sacred song, a prosperous wand –
       Though even as I catch up, I leave behind
       The bears that never crept into my mind.

WEEKEND IN THE SMOKIES

What is a vacation? On a clouded afternoon
I sit on a balcony watching the motionless Swiss valley,
and the back of my collar drifts with the same mild breeze
that woos the dirt downhill. I am thirty-five miles
from home, the others are shopping in Gatlinburg.
Behind me in the lodge I can hear water
crooning out of taps; here on the porch
wasps sweep, swoop, miss my pencil.

Distant motors reach me, cars in the distance
glisten a time and die. Football, the World Series
result elsewhere, but this is change, this scene,
this immobility suddenly in my life:
a bulge of smoke far off, a car cursing
gravel on an unseen road, old barns, divided land,
and only the wasps really and truly move
through the world's whitenesses and fear of rain.

For only a moment, not used to waiting, I wait,
I wait with the hills – then, restless, ask that breeze, that caw,
that edge of sun on the far slope lighting its green,
tree by tree, not questions only but favors:
How does the drying blood within me join us?
What river are we? *Take place in my poem.*
By the time the others return, I am bent to my paper,
busy again, professional, and dying.

THE FENCE

It seems to me I'm always at work on my fence,
my wife says "never." Truth is between us.
She notices that the dog gets out. I think
of my torn hands and all I have laid – barbed wire,
        the piles of brush, the staves,

logs, boards, barrels, old tires, millions of leaves,
stray bricks, great sheets of tin, abandoned doors,
everything I can scrounge in the fields around
our single inhabited lot – to keep our dog inside,
        and it's all useless.

He delights in the game, fakes that he's my helper,
inspects the new arrangements and then trots off.
Intent on thorns, bugs, barbs, compulsive hammerer,
manning my wire stretcher, my hands cursing,
        I forget to watch,

and there he is, out at another gap,
browsing about the bush, dung-deep in smells.
I figure the signs, glare at where he's squeezed through.
First it was under the wire, then between but
        low, now higher. When will he jump?

There's less and less to sniff on the other side.
Machines have ploughed the trees and sketched roads.
It's all mud to the west and south where a new suburb
will lodge its coffins. Troilus, having no views
        on these lively social questions,

still longs to escape and for me to discover he's gone,
climb wire, then yell "COME!" to his deafening Doberman joy.
(He sometimes responds to my bass; to my baritone, never.)
Into stickers I stalk, catch, beat, drive him back
          through the gate, happy, loved.

Over a year we've been at this now. He has
an acre or more: why does he need the world?
Well, why do I fence him in when he never runs off?
But he might, he might, and he's stupid about cars,
          just smart about me. No matter:

we've entered the closing phase, with chicken wire
I attack the final gaps, and in half a year
we leave for good, the house comes down, and the yard
will be leveled, this maze of barbs that I put up here
          in all my living pain

will never be scratched by human hand, but a gold bulldozer
will push it over, scrunch it up, shove it aside,
bury it under dirt, with the terminal trees
and the rest of the violent obscure life that now
          composes our private plot.

Waved Night (Minneapolis)

POEM, PARTLY FOUND, PARTLY FUMBLED

Well, living in Minneapolis has its rewards:
only a little smoke in the lungs, the Guthrie,
that river lurking symbolically about,
and where else could a fan letter to Carl Eller blow into my back yard?

310 Yadkin St.
Raleigh, N.C. 27609
April 23, 1971

Dear Mr. Carl Eller,

I have always admired the way you play
football. You dumped so many Q.B.'s I can't
count them. I love to play rough games, thats
why I picked football. And I like rough and
tough players like you.

Your greatgreatgreat fan,

Edward L. Frazelle

P.S. Please send picture

We should ask at once the salient questions:

Why was the letter written on Shakespeare's birthday?
And mailed from Raleigh?
Is *yadkin* a slip for *bodkin*?
Account for the pervasive Elizabethan motifs,
      the devious allusions to the gravedigger scene in
      Hamlet, the internal rhyme scheme (*rough-tough,*
      can't-count, way-play, picked-picture) suggestive of
      Jacobean intrigue.
  Explain the numbers. Break the code. Admit
      that Carl Eller is the ghost of Edward's father.
      ("Please send picture," of course, is what Hamlet
      keeps telling *his* father.)
Why, then, has he permitted his son to be worn to a frazelle?
      Above all, why did he throw the letter away?

The mysterious Upper Midwest!
                    The inscrutable Carl Eller!

BEYOND REMINISCENCE

"Remember when . . .?" But to be beyond reminiscence,
beyond caring when whatever it was happened,
or whether it happened, cold to the old friend's face,

knowing the distant past for a delusion,
thirty years, forty years ago, all false,
all a dead image, as tonight the talk,

turning, ripped up ancient ping-pong, mean
words, fast friends I let go long ago,
let go regret, too, and lived elsewhere, had to,

had to to weather. Not that that's forgotten –
the childish stress is busy in my brain,
warmth still encrusts the futile kind old fools,

the adolescent cities, resolves, first loves;
but tonight's window, like a prow at sea
disclaiming origins, touches tonight's snow,

and it's the present cold goads me to go.

BLIZZARD

Still snowing on April 9th, April 10th.
Figure it will snow into August, snow to become
our permanent condition, this rush of flakes

under the streetlamp our true element,
our air. Someone is turning us upside down
in his hand, showing to still astonished children

our snow-baffled world, our fiction of falling snow
as of a glass believed in, peopled, shaken,
a curiosity on an adult's shelf –

that it *could* snow somewhere like that, flurry and drift
into a person's life, into *ours*!
We have all been blown into the glass of April.

THIS TOO

And to imagine this too, this
nondescript moment, here in untroubled
Syracusa

not or not really the actual agi-
tation by the embattled gate, the Red
Sea parting in wonder

but nothing, only an afternoon in
drydock, nothing, no detail seeking
to be better established or –

till the mind says, *Seize it, seize*
the day, this one, in all its hilarious humdrum, even
this one, seize it!

And then, then the coloring light, and a grieving
face it flayed in the moment's dense and
puzzled suffusion,

whatever the pain, are good and compose
in Syracuse. Later a drifting snow-thoughted wretch
may recur to this.

DISTANT COUSINS

The snow isn't worried.
Flakes like swarming bees beat about the gaslight,
small white things dropped out of the night.
We come from different families.

Mother of snow, my life,
grow next to this beautiful child, take on its
color and softness before it folds its
water and leaves us.

This trunk, my heart,
is almost always already halfway filled
with poor relations. *Bring me to my knees.*
Come through the glass, snow, muffle and dance me.

EVENING

any number of
green, clinging
lives out there

I lean my
withering arms
on the window sill
almost sure of
outlasting all that
summer vigor
this time
this time

next time
's not so sure
sooner or later
most of their lownesses
or their indifferent
populous progenies
will still be true to their
creeping schedules

when for these
moral, these
shortsighted eyes
tonight's half-moon
has inadvertently,
lightly, loosely –
no appeal, no
Red Cross, rescue –
evaded notice

ZERO

Cold, zero, lower, I walk
what is left, my living room,
turn on the light and absorb
the shock of my life, my life

comes at me in waves, it
is hideous, beautiful, tonight
as always it lurked, sprang
so that I turned, was struck, was

ice and ice-
cold, forgetting that you
fit in the room I live
as zero, light, shock, my life

FIRE-LIFE

After a while the lives about me make
a wall of flames against which, scorched and laddered,
I lean, and haul my fire-life, and climb.

The whole sky crackles as I read my book.
At a sharp word floors crumple, and a huge roar
runs with the red night across the room.

What is violence? Can the burned bush enrich me?
While one self wanes, steers blind, despairs, and rescues,
a smaller ghost within me still sits tight.

This is the way I learn love, flare, grow old.
Yea, though I sleep, though dark hours, days, dim me,
my house is eaten through and through with light.

PARTY

1. Undertones

    All this idle talk, no talker idling,
everyone on, just done, or waiting turn,
or not waiting, into the melee piling
voices of fear, question, voices of scorn,
voices that bruise, that flare up and put down,
slow stubborn speech, or speech that's glib and coarse,
voice that insists, that quavers, that breaks tune,
the tired voice that can't stop, my own voice
contending, contending, over background noise,
rude arguers, specious arguments, foul air,
these decent, brutal people, that beneath their poise
in speech there spills an aria of despair.

    Why do we do it? Just to touch, with talk,
and whip, a little, where cold words can't wake?

2. Drink

    Slowly the cell door closes, letting you into
forests tremendously your own. The tide
of trivial opposition pulls aside,
hushes its agony to let you through
into . . . into feeling what is finally true.
Love like an odor streams from your quickened side,
flooding the room the world, where no guilts hide,
where nothing quivers that might question you.

Only, only those voices dragging down
your vision; in the mirror as you pass,
your face is wearing someone else's frown:
pain, not love, palpable in the glass,
which lies, lies, like this whole crooked town . . . .
Sleep slowly takes you from the cross.

3. After

After a party, the memory of babble,
faces contending for the bright spot of recall
brighten in lamplight and give way to next ones:
Mind, tender and remorseless, lets them slip by.
Figures group, gesture, dissolve, rooms are augmented
by entrances, by heads struck back in laughter.
One after another, quietly peering,
friends bend over the buffet, their lit hands reach.

Like images convene and push my brain
over the vivid evening, drag awareness
through thick air, souls desperate to get through.
The sense of the dark street leans against the glass.
Soon sleep, action, sleep will dispel them
and all these strangers drift off, not through doors.

AFFIRMATIVE ACTION

1 a.m. Friday night:
       asleep we both
wake to the big sound (rock – "*a little love*")
blaring across the street. It isn't the first time, so,
indignant, robe about me, I steer my drooping
eyes in the dragon's direction.

        The lights are all on
where the seven children, ages from two to twelve,
live with their welfare mother. She goes on trips
(one to a bowling convention in Las Vegas),
and I've hardly seen her around in the months she's lived here.
Because of that, and its being so dark, I mistake
the big black woman sitting on the opposite stoop
(along with the gentle woman who resides there)
for someone else. I say, "*That's a lotta noise, isnit?*"
"*We like it,*" she counters. Judging the skirmish lost
in that quarter, I shake my head and mention
the hour, then make for the lighted door across
the street. I ring, no answer. Now, gradually,
over the blare I hear her faintly saying,
"*Nobody home,*" and realize who she is.

"*I wonder if you could turn it down,*" I ask
reasonably. She turns to the gentle soul
beside her and says mock-friendly, "*What do you think?*
Should we turn it down?" The gentle soul says, "*I think so.*"
Reluctantly, to prove she doesn't have to,
she swaggers into the street, telling me I wouldn't
have said word one if there hadn't been between us
a difference of color. I say it's a matter of noise,
not color, but she goes on about a party
the other night at some white people's house down the street.

"*I didn't complain*," she says. "*Why not?*" I say.
"*I wish you would. If **I** hear **their** noise **I** will.*
*If **we** have a party and the noise disturbs you, **tell** us.*"

"*Oh you*," she says, moving into the music,
"*you jes' growin' old on the corner.*"

NOCTURNE

Now night unclosets
its box of far noises
and sets them out for each

waker, worker, or even
the long breathers, whose vaults, love,
lie open

to forms of the waves' subsiding,
chords of the cricket's
bow, the bruised sound

of that train in the distance,
or here at hand, near,
the breeze riffling trees.

What do we mean? they all
ask as they measure
night for their listeners.

COMPANIONS

Reaching out from this center
I aspire to touch
lightning and distance.

There now, I have them
cupped in my hand, though my dog
would howl if he knew

if he knew I unleash them
nightly in poems
beyond my cry, **Come!**

creatures walking
unimaginable moons,
breathless, without grievance,

not caring whether
their source, light years
behind them in the left-for-dark,

calms a dog, is dead,
or, struck, risen from sleep,
turns on a brighter lamp.

HOME MOVIE

At two a.m. or so
in a darkened room
I run through yesterday's rushes.
Guilt and grief and I
excise the trivial, the unpatterned.
My name is stamped on the anxious moments –
more than my name, what I am –
and on others.

Then at last, those blurred images
dissolved in sleep, the film
is filed in the dark red vaults
for future distribution
at uncertain times and feelings.
Ignorant librarian,
I chug my scarred catalogue
through the waved night.

New day, new reel, new life.
Author, actor, censor,
I take and re-take
these mis-edited streets and people,
the fumes and lives
with whom I am co-featured,
not knowing even the film's name
or what I represent.

OUTCRIES

Those outcries in the night we used to wake to
before we moved to Hopkins – can you hear them
even here, even in winter with the windows closed?

I can remember waking in the dark,
hearing the bands of neighborhood blades blow by
or pause at the corner, uncertain which still street

to wander pointlessly down, making their point
at three in the morning. Then when the last crisp
voice had followed the flow, we would hear an occasional

car hold at the corner and as it turned
a kind of diaphanous abstract private film
swept over our ceiling. Like people in Plato's cave

we might turn to each other or not, not knowing exactly
what we had seen, what beast we had nearly started,
its motive or source, these lives thrown out at odd hours

by the city whose natural life is flame, around us
all soothed by night by now, and only waiting to
explode sooner or later into broad daylight.

ENCORE

Arrived at my desk this early hour,
I audition what is on hand: a suffering car,
the wind performing through relaxed trees,

my wife sleeps, the dog scratches his bed,
the newsboy tosses his weight at my door
and draws his steps away. Bent on words,

I acknowledge this universe I have devised
by waking up, this silence idling, this brightness.
Sleep has turned me into a theater again,

robed for that radiant play, my muddled life.
Before the anguish resumes, sipping strong colors,
I push back my deep desk chair and applaud softly.

THE CARD PLAYERS (CÉZANNE)

They must have died sixty, seventy years ago;
the painter's dead, the painting's in the Louvre.
All night, these years, eternal in my room,
they ponder the next discard – study in light,
in hat-shapes, ease, endurance . . .

Day comes, another card drops from my hand.

CRICKET

In the local blightment
that shrinks below our apartment
where sand and gravel
undergird urban travel,
a single cricket
saws from his scruffy thicket
that repetitious number
his legs can't misremember.
Lonely and metered,
not in the least embittered,
probably unacquainted
with lushness, self centered
in what he has found
of ground and sound,
not caring if cousins from hedges
now reside in garages
or whether the bugs might bite better
with some catchier method.
All his few days
he just does what he does
wherever he is.
We'd hate it, we
squeak out our harmony
dissonantly.

Strenuous Life

PERSONAL

An open statement to you Mary. L. Olson
Buttrick or what other names you have
been using here. The time of truth is
running out for you. Your debts are
yours alone. What you are and have been
here and elsewhere will follow you and
Cindy no matter whether Kansas,
Flagstaff or New Mexico. You know what
you did to Omar Heupert and John Olson.
       – Tucumcari (N.M.) *News*, August 22, 1974

Your names are many but your friends are few,
Mary L. Olson Buttrick, most long flown.
The time of truth is running out for you.

Whatever names you have been using, you
Remember now your debts are yours alone.
Your debts are many but your friends are few.

Rent's due, and retribution's overdue,
For what you are and have been, what you've done.
The time of truth is running out for you.

And now just Cindy's left of all that crew.
You know what you did to Omar and to John.
Your trails are many but your friends are few.

In Kansas, Flagstaff or New Mexico,
No matter how far you and Cindy run,
The time of truth is running out for you.

This open statement is addressed to you
In hopes you'll see the parlous path you're on.
Your words are many but your friends are few.
The time of truth is running out for you.

VISITING

Whenever we go visiting, my wife and I,
responding to invitation or at loose ends,
they pop up at us from rugs or out from doors,
        the small people of our friends.

Chubby-palmed, hands front for balance, swinging, tongue at
lips, they stare with faintly troubled assurance,
not knowing entirely how to interpret
        these large people of their parents.

We too are nonplussed, by the aplomb with which
at two or ten they recapitulate
one progenitor's jaw and the other's bent
        for love, long reach, or hate.

Already their remorseless games project
a lover's style or tantrum politics.
Three kids in a yard describe "American man
        (flourished 1996)."

Still, we are bound to grow bored as, through their charm,
Dad's roped-in pride, Mom's competence offspringwise,
the bloodshot film of evolution rolls
        before our childless eyes.

THE COUPLE

Moved, but afraid, to part,
he darts out, jumpy, like a riddled nerve,
she stays, assured the moment asks for verve,
their gross fine art,

frayed and decayed, played out,
all touches out of season, out of phase,
evenings of separation, abstract days
beaten about

like an old citadel
with the blown corpses of old jokes, stoned scenes,
bland reconstructions of what no one means
though both can tell

not with the voice but with
crabbed veins how evenly the anguish splits
their double animal, its movements, its
stealth become myth

that like an open book
waits to be taken up or not – who cares? –
yet even now can be torn unawares
just by a look.

SIMPLY A RECORD

This is simply a record
of one of your famous drunks, the laughs, the faces,
the good time had by all. You'll remember the date,
the drunk, the occasion, the tissue – the *toilet* – paper
strung from the trees, and how it began, the famous
coat too long in the sleeves, the party's roaring
start, the good-natured joshing. This is a record
of that, simply of that, and of what happened next,
the famous contest to see whose legs had the spring
to jump over Eiffels of cans in the backyard dark, the famous
blazer you drenched that night, the famous question I put
in front of our famous friends, and the stalking drunken
high-hearted hollow swagger among drained bottles
that led you to land on the famous ankle that's still
not right, and this is the famous poem that came
out of that night, my anger, and, honestly, saintlike
patience.

ACKNOWLEDGMENT

Ernie, bound to me by agony,
remember mine (my agony!) in the subway
that winter evening something deep in my
          belly exploded?

Sixteen, just weeks at war, baffled and painstruck I
couldn't retch, wouldn't howl, the spear kept twisting
inside me, you helped me up thousands of steps, you
          saved my life then.

Extravagantly resourceful, found a taxi
to hearse me home in, bursting into
my parents' Saturday party, who gaped and phoned doctors
          to come fix me.

They did, better – it was all a blessing.
Not so, months later, when – *I wasn't there*! – they
cut your infected leg off, and the rest of you
          began twisting.

PLAYGROUND

The bus I slump back home on every week,
after the hour with the analyst,
shakes to the end of its run a few blocks on,
then stops beside a playground and shuts down.
It is four o'clock on Monday afternoon.

Deep in, but suddenly out of, my own hard times,
I watch skip rope, clap hands, punch, clamber, wrestle,
the witty, small usurpers. The fence, chain link,
lets in my eyes, but a wall of shrieks and whistles
keeps me from any of their words. I sit alone

and admire these jumping, howling puppies, pick out
the solitary, finger-biting one I was,
and turn my eyes over the whole tableau:
there is the force of what I now try to say
at three o'clock on Monday afternoons –

dredged up, patterned out, on the asphalt court,
stage after stage, my own disorder danced.
And I am clean when the bus driver snaps
his stub into the gutter, climbs to his seat,
spins his glass of money, and we waggle home.

YOUNG MAN'S SONG

When to the night of sleep
You bring your single love
And the breaking hours keep
Tides of curious life –
Wind and traveled wave
Idling in the moon's steep
Unwatching eye – I wonder
What's it not to wife
Weather in this under
Apart from that above,
Not to hold up the art
Of the infinite bride and groom
To this reality?
Cloak torn from the heart
And love at large in the room
And every alien form
Effaced or at sea,
Put on the grace of sin
Before the gasped alarms,
And come awake within
My only overnight arms.

HARRY

My first boss in a real civilian job –
fat, spectacles, suspendered – gorged too rich
one lunchtime, writhed with chest pains, and, in tones
as of the last trump, called for his bookkeeper wife:
"Get Hazel, I'm checkin' out."

These years, when scholars' rumbles revel down,
that image of mortality returns.
Harry stayed on; later, I chucked the job,
checked out for California and the word-life.
How long ago did Harry pay the bill?

REMINISCENCE OF A CALIFORNIA AFFAIR

I

What I remember clearly is the deaf psychiatrist
nodding gravely – not grasping, as I grasp now,
what I really wanted, figuring I had to have come for

"help" or comfort, and stealing behind his frieze
of professional effort at clarification. My part of our talk
spread out on the couch he lounged on; the darkly paneled

living room let in little Pacific light;
but I saw that what I had climbed to uncover he wouldn't
tell me, trained to deflect question with question,

to give nothing up, not even the time of day.
I had made a mistake, had thought of him as a neighbor,
of hers at least, of theirs – "*Oh **David**,*" she would say,

"*David is **wonderful***" and lean back into her giggle
on the hot drive to Mexico City – someone next door
with a degree in trouble like theirs or simply

a scarfed Bay Area shaman whose plants and daughter
were just of the size and suburb. Foiled and resigned,
for politeness' sake I pretended to scrawl new messages.

II

It was twenty-five years ago this coming summer,
and the questions I put have never been met – for all
I've heard, the whole crowd may be dead, while hundreds of leagues

to the east, and still, in a dark room, crumpling my bits
of paper, I go on rasping the figures, asking,
"*From what you know of their lives, whose side should I take,*

or even if I must decide, tell me something about these
strangers of mine." David still gravely nods
and in a voice that only I can hear

asks gently, "*Why is it a problem for you?*"
Suddenly, as by paper lanterns, I see my
whole strenuous life since strung on these futile questions.

MY SAD CAPTAIN

Face in the mirror, puffed, aging,
why do you drag me round these walls –
parties, poetry readings, bleedings?
        The pace appalls.

Or is it the stealth that kills
your synchronized, competent squads
that only years ago, we know,
        drilled like a god's?

At times, or over a time, you'd think
you'd think to put the troops at ease.
Shouldn't you shout, *Enough! Fall out!* –
        Or are you these?

AHEAD OF SCHEDULE

It takes time at least for
Time, I thought, to
warp the legs, crack
the smile, flab
the white face's
creases

       safe at worst for another
       twelvemonth surely

when Time, old
fattener, old
thinner, came lurching
across the stricken dancefloor
to crab my hand.

DEAD HAND

Come back, my hand; reclaim those agile ways,
your careless glides and strains, the easy lift,
light touch, and thoughtless grasp. You grieve me now,
stiff and loath to bend, fingers that hardly
stir of their own accord, wrist that declines
to flex further than neutral, parallel.
Don't you remember when you were a hand,
my hand, my left, lapsed hand? (*I'm talking to you!*)

I thought we'd established long ago that you were
the helping hand, trained to the trifling tasks:
holding, steadying, straightening, balancing – fixing
for clever Dexter here to put the point to –
the Shoelace Adjutant, co-Button Handler.
I've saved you, over the years, two major missions –
card-dealing, opening jars – made you my Time-
Bearer, named my Best Supporting Limb . . .

But don't expect to garner any long-term benefits
by your present genuinely scandalous behavior. True,
you have my attention now: I bathe you, nurse,
douse you with lotion, massage, cajole your joints,
inspect your line, your desiccated skin,
watch ruefully your first hand-baby steps,
press the wrist softly to remind you of
lost spools and trains of action, and rewind

an elegiac bandage round the splint
that holds your moves in bondage. But, hand, soon,
your dereliction dwindled, tracks re-opened,
the last twinges and tremors mere mementos,
I'll treat you to as thorough a forgetting
as perfect parts deserve, taking their place
in the full aging ensemble, an autumn piece
fluted and horned, ripe for grander regretting.

OLD MAN IN WAITING ROOM

I have run by all the doctors.

Once, fathers, powers, they set my broken arms,
performed, prescribed at will. I was in their hands. I believed.
If I could be saved, they would save me.
And I lived.

Now, just as passive on the other side,
I let their young hands take soundings.
They know what to do with bones
but my great experience is against them.

That file that that bored nurse sets by the doctor's hand –
what can it know of this running?

ACCIDENT REPORT

All that I felt was falling
but which way?
Trying to see but the color
of falling was black
and tremendous noise.

Then when it stopped and pain, light, figuring
restored a road
down which we still moved slowly,
parts of what I partly am
began their aching messages.

For three days protest
waved its indignant signs in me
and I kept going over and over
that death, that forespasm
for what it could tell me

of the permanent blindness,
as if to be aware
but wholly unknowing
were like not being. I know dying
but am none the wiser.

MARLY

Friend, of a brightness nothing merely
human could wither, I grieve to recall it's
more than a year today since the cancer
        wasted your radiance.

Though when you died I was more than ten countries
distant, I still half smile to remember
that once, in your illness, on my way to see you,
        I wrecked my old Rambler.

Grim joke, that wreckage, all I could tender,
nothing then, nothing now, to ease that pain.
I wrote a poem about it, pretended I
        knew about dying.

We both were learning, but your comprehensive
came up first, mine still pending.
I just want to say, as if you could hear me,
        Marly, I've missed you.

MÉNAGE À TROIS

Ménage à trois, which we
and our mortality
must share as with a guest:

the thing we've somehow made,
bland but to be obeyed,
breaks even breakers' rest;

and though it tears, it stays,
though the rag it is betrays
breath, though it mock,

it argues like a past
for what, though frail, will last.
Paper covers rock.

THE NEXT LARGEST QUESTIONS

The days go by like beads
strung on immediate issues, nights from some deep
the largest powers come crawling through my sleep
to carve their creeds.

Caught between those and these,
I have no time for the next largest questions.
Ignored in life, quite settled in my fictions,
they seethe at ease

till, like some ancient Evil
that, after aeons' inward burning, burst
violently down vales soon seen as cursed,
a rock upheaval

wrenches them from between
my sleep and business, in the blasted space
of leering daylight forces me to face
what my words mean.

NIGHTFALL NEAR LOUISVILLE

Flying at sunset into clouds' dark ravines,
                night to the east and down,
we find submerging is the only means
                to turn up a town.

That heaven to which, with pious, lifted eyes,
                the propertied make prayer
locates itself beneath our folding skies,
                bright, dark, down there.

Holding a breath or engine as we sink
                to our essential black,
we realize that Hell is how we think
                of falling back.

That we should come, seems crooked at the least,
                and worth the weather's frown,
after so grand a climb, to be the beast
                with two ways down.

PENDING

The highway sounds
flare in my ears at night.

Across these grain-crossed fields,
across Minnesota,

reduced to the insect hrum
of pure migration,

they come in folds
neither to warn nor to promise

a creature whose pending
has learned to abide them.

DRIVING THROUGH TENNESSEE

Flail, farmer; swerve, crow.
My route parts and forgets you.

VILLANELLE ON NEARING SEVENTY

Who could have dreamt that it would come to this
when I was young and could gauge nothing clear?
Step after step it's been just hit or miss.

When, in New York, wary of close and kiss,
I ran from love but learned to ride that fear,
could I have dreamt that it would come to this?

Cold, drafted, inexperienced at bliss,
I trained to joust with jostle, jest and jeer.
Step after step, there too, just hit or miss.

World travel crisped my wings, like Icarus'.
I hoped by falling I might tune my ear,
but never dreamt that it would come to this.

Four decades deeper into the abyss
have not diminished my desire to steer.
Step after step, always just hit or miss.

What if I'd guessed, back then, the body's criss-
cross love could take these turnings year by year?
Would I have dreamt that it could come to this?
Step after step after step, just hit or miss.

Roots and Epitaphs

I. Home

BASSETT'S CREEK

Minneapolis

Sometimes if you're awake late at night
you hear the boxcars switching over by Bassett's
Creek – delicate thuds hooded by dark

and distance, kept from the lives of all who are near but
sleeping, unless they switch softly the images
whose coupling makes a dream. If you're awake

and coupling, then these gentle night-drenched booms,
the far park's echoes of the pounding blood
about you, seem chorale. But if you sit

alone, sleepless, indeterminate, the tremors come
as stoppages, as dooms, from here to there
trackless, the creek and you estranged, still.

BURNING THE LEAVES

Embattled, -broiled, this patch of smoke-torn field
all one engages: it will bury us.
I had scruples, wondered if reporting events
justly would jeopardize those whose events they were,
as if – Let each man, prisoned as he is,
examine his premises. One series might read
New York, Winchester, Asbury Park, another
would fix San Francisco between two Souths.
Only, embarrassed at acting like a tourist,
I clicked my camera prematurely. Light
decides what to rake next. All we can do,
assured of dark goggles and whirling snow,
is wait and bow, as toward the emperor's party.

PROGRAM

One of the humpers, man: makes riddles, walls.
Lately, just within these three or four days,
the brown winter has come viciously alive,

its buds and shades eating into my resignation.
Last year's leaves are still unhinging. This would be, I thought,
a promising area for future development –

not, that is, the land but the allegory,
with the same motion opening the screen door and casting
back on the whole back yard, hungering dog,

the melee of kids in the alley, a theatrical glance.
Margin of error: none. To make the identical
golf-swing every time, but from altered lies.

GENIUS LOCI

"*Here*," said the epitaph, not "*rolled around*":
a person of this place. But by nineteen-now
motors have made almost everyone non-indigenous,

and no soul has a history, just a career.
Over the din of bulldozer and freeway,
above my rant, your spool of airport noise,

can anyone hear the Genius-of-the-Place?
Taxes aside, what does it cost to live here?
But once the ground is leveled, the trees upripped,

how can you call a subdivision a place?
When you dig up the chthonic deities,
they decompose: that is their property.

THREE-TURKEY CANYON

Canyon de Chelly, Arizona

A canyon wall. Under it – not below,
but under the wall – the old ones hung their towns
like hives or pumpkins, pierced in the sandstone facing

masks of the many-shadowed cliff, and made
of their brief tenure by these masterful rocks
a grace to weave, fire, dance. About that year

Normans building Winchester, Monreale,
stretched the stone upward, then let the cracked light through.
Here the gods, meager givers, squatters, squinters,

gave toothache, backache, plague, drought, a steep life,
foreclosure: the wall held, the people crumbled
elsewhere – I would, too – but kept their gods.

MESA VERDE

Where are they now? The sun is in the eye.
The landscape has become a vast museum.
The sacredness I feel in others' lives

I've learned from aging, not from agriculture.
Also from Wordsworth, whom I take seriously:
great English shaman, with a feel for graveyards.

Shopping for wonders, I, with other tourists,
applaud these pueblo architects: *Good show*!
having no gods but what the cliffs throw back,

no branch that flames. From where I write I can make out,
twenty-odd miles to the south, Shiprock in smog,
Notre Dame of the desert, plug, nothing to me.

THE TURN

Not trees but *like* trees once, rooted, placed,
migrant as vegetation is, transhumant
from crag to plain, men guided by their flocks

to where the grass still gives itself, or following
the musk-ox or the yielding glacier: so,
obedient to the beating of the rain,

dry beds engorging, or whatever brings
the earth by labor to sustain its blind
co-breathers.   And then the tree got up,

disowned its mountain, learned to make mistakes,
said me, invented a new kind of leaf,
thought much on old attachments, and felt sick.

II. Abroad

EXERCISE

Mornings, mortars, Missouri – waking to men
rattling their mess-gear on the mist-diamonded hillside
till the mist cleared and we could make out the boneless old

shack, our target, trained our aiming circles
on it, trained the guns by our aiming circles,
and blew up the landscape. It was basic training.

Later we brought the same talents to bear
on a German hillside, the mortars shooting blind
from a declivity over the heads of observers

(including this observer) crouched in a pillbox.
The war was over, this an exercise
simply to keep our twitching, aimless hand in.

THE BOHEMIANS

In the Bohemian Grove, where actors, bankers,
brokers hobnobbed with cabinet members, justices,
former and future Presidents, and hundreds-of-years-old

classic redwoods, all that counted was eminence.
There, like a slave on the Palatine, I watched
emperors at their ease; midsummer nights,

drank with polite old lifers in their cups, or helped
aged Gelett Burgess shuffle home.
One Sunday I fetched his paper for Herbert Hoover,

who sat at breakfast ringed by twenty moguls;
when his hand went to his pocket, twenty hands went to theirs;
embarrassed, I refused the tip but kept the scene.

PAYSAGES DE GENÈVE

Excursions from Geneva – the Petit Salève,
from which L. whispered she'd "cast" herself if . . .
Voltaire's Ferney and its command of Mont Blanc, of us,

that day we took our place among the few
in Western letters to have looked for a needle in a haystack;
bicycle rides all fall by Byron's lake,

the leaves so bright they hurt my eyes remembering;
and through the hip-deep snow one Sunday little
Bouchard led me trudging above Montreux . . .

Jean-Jacques, John Calvin, these have been my chains,
along with the torn woman who wouldn't applaud
passionate sound Fürtwängler somehow found there.

COMBRAY

But the real city's inside. Those glowing others,
whose grids I've spent half my life trying to know –
for what? so I could get around? (*around*?) –

encode alternative nervous systems. Even
the Texas town for which a past and plan
emerge as our maimed car seeks its mechanic

bears more than passing likeness to a person,
and when I tilt the blinds on my ten cities
(not counting tourist capitals, French hill towns,

lit streets learned one night only), they empower
that charged imagination of a self that Proust,
augmenting his great-aunt's house, called Combray.

PROVENCE

To take hold of this life – *"Life! Life!"* – as those
awakening Edwardians used to exclaim – to find
with Holmes (with Hyde!) its secret, with Conrad and Ford its

narrative system, with that unwatched pea-watcher monk the mechanism of
Life, the locked room, but in the air about us,
impenetrable, some movement in the dusk

beckoning young Joyce from the lurid doorways,
young Eliot, Lawrence – till their appeased experience
becomes the root of mine, more than the island

I happened to be born on, my fifty years
a graft upon Van Gogh's perception of tormented
blossoming boughs, across the road ruins

of Roman reason. Eight kilometers on,
behind strange lumpy hills the lords of Baux
dispassionately toss Life down my own cliffs.

EN ROUTE

Moving to other matters, as we must,
and while we can. The books and buildings blow
by, like the wind, life always aspiring

to the condition of images, swept in turn
past window, weekend, out of my small hand's
reach. I ask nightly of poems, *Whose voice*

wants to be mine? But something, I know, is not quite
right with the rhythm, the tone – the truth – is off.
I am trying to write all the poems I've brought

with me because it's too hard hearing my life,
no one is listening beside me, and the museum
moves on to other matters, as it must.

ROADS

San Francisco

The wilderness is still our metaphor
even in the city. My mind, constantly wandering,
happens on its romantic rivers but has to

arrange its possibilities in roads.
When I had no car, freedom for me was going
out Pine Street as far as it ran, Seattle or Kansas

it didn't matter, just clear of my cramped room and job.
On the edge of the city's life, I wanted its engines
to throw me off, to hurl me out to some truth:

even in Marin County I might find my poem.
I wanted, down all my roads, to make of some wild
wording of things the stone of my own life.

III. Around

SKELETON

The skeleton lies in a single bed, beyond
caress, beneath contempt, its lime waiting
the painless next stage of the cancer. Skin
gone, organs dismantled, it detects
(like Charlie Chan: *"Murderer make one mistake"*)
the mask has all this time been *underneath*.

But, Charlie, if the truth is dissolution,
if what we come to is community
always dispersing, I am content to let
the worms or medical students probe my suntan –
on this condition, that the step they do
mulch earth or tune a soul, help me at last,
fallen through history, to amount to something.

UNDERSTUDIES

Staten Island

Above the town the former persons work
out of it. Here in the family plot, where stones
announce the family acts, a listless cast

unbosoms. Agamemnon forgets his lines.
Helen has kept that superb bone structure. Of all
our places, the graveyard posts no mirrors. We couldn't

find Uncle Bill last time, we never found
the grave of Hamlin Garland. They must have been learning
new cues, new business: just de- or recomposing

probably commands all one's attention – what it
means to slip into something else, a role
that calls for slighter talents, but concentrated . . .

VIEWING THE REMAINS

Rome

Self-pitying epitaphs of great small men:
"Here lies One Whose Name was writ in Water."
That was before the tombstone script gave way

to the obituary notice, when graveyards were
the same community differently arranged,
a choir beside the choir. Then maybe Keats,

knowing he'd been abstracted from the village,
a chance voice caught briefly above the crowd,
felt the tiered city as a huge moist page

to sop up who he was, whoever he was.
Jarring what Shelley called *"so sweet a place,"*
the eternal Roman rattle now writes on his bones.

THE JOYCES AT HOME

Zürich

Now they've moved Nora near him, let them go
earthwise wherever. To whom can they matter, these mounds?
The great bear effigy we saw in Iowa, cleared for

everyone's climb and look, connected more.
But why should any of it arrest us so,
except as burial practice, getting set

to learn, near woods and water, schemes of repose?
What's helped before, this side – the taking measure
of worlds we don't know quite what to make of – may

still count for something when the final oddness
comes like a bear and calls, as the dark loses
lucidity, "*Move nearer, Nora . . .whoever . . .*"

TURNOVER COUNTRY

New Mexico

Turnover country – that's what it's all so hard to
realize we're in till earthfall, that no engine,
no stone, averts the turning, that a brightness

flakes from our lips continually to compose
the joys we die of and pursue heartlong.
Only, like boulders belched out on a plain

by heaving mountains, we want to be for a time
a little remarked, left in the young ones' way
to speak in cipher of those forces that

impelled us, blind yet balanced, to this gravity.
As for the thought, that costs our lives to learn,
unless the form is beautiful, no one will care.

LOOKING AHEAD

Every event is irreversible, nothing
at all is central, final. It's just between
the boards of our book that Life, given

this melancholy color, lavishes these
years to bring out our values, and then, done, finished,
pages close, book is returned to shelf,

the Reader goes on reading. Soon, like a god,
powerless to alter what was never fixed
till now, moment on moment trains its eye

in the strict university of what's here,
as if we went on living, as if Life itself
were human, as if ours hadn't been the crucial case.

AMBITION

To make, to have made, a difference; things as they come
to swerve in going; by a word, a son,
one set in the field, to turn light into grain,

to green the shadows. To be able to say, beyond
sweetness or cant, as of love's surge or a farmscape,
This is the golden time, and let it be.

RECOIL

Images of disaster thread my mind:
I am pinned beneath the ice, a centipede
furs out of the faucet into the glass
I drink from in the dark. At Mesa Verde
a woman said, *"Last year we went to the Grand Canyon.*
We saw a young man, taking a picture, take one
step too many." For days he haunted me:
on the way down, to become reconciled,
camera and all?
               Or else to die of detail,
office by office.
               Come, fabulous morning,
unravel these false images, make my life
of horn and tedium, dream me as you will.

Academic Affairs

Classroom

TEACHING

A man trying to hold onto nine balloons –
they keep bumping into each other and away
from his lunging arms, they are squeezing out,
slipping out, with strange panicky rubbing
noises, and he's losing them, he's losing them all.

Even without a wind he loses them all
and they bounce, in uneasy vectors, onto the walk
where the breeze stirs and passersby kick them
so that they rouse and drift over the lawn
and a sparrow pecks them: they burst, and the man is gone.

ENGLISH CLASS

Today my students orally report
each on the topic of his or her research.

The nervous, swarthy boy reaches the lectern
in a white shirt and has nothing to say but: "Okay."
Then, on guard, in one breath:
"Thetitleofmypaperis'TheCourt-MartialofBillyMitchell'."
Overmadeup, dark Miss Tinsel slinks without notes
to the front of the room and tells how they ratified
the Ladies' Suffrage Amendment.
Tall, thin, stern, the scholarship basketball player
speaks on bees, how they swarm, their social life, and what happens
to the superannuated queens. Next, a blonde doll,
her heavy face clutched by her hair, losing her looks at eighteen,
irrepressibly shallow, explains in two minutes the ethical profundities
                                        of Confucianism.
Taoists, she says, were for spirits. (*Me too, me too.*)

The Southern voice carouses up and down,
the stylized tones of these shrewd fantasists –
boys, girls, masks of youth, puppy masks
– in some weird way they are choosing their lives!
Deep-voiced, big ears, brown eyes, dark brows under crewcut,
gives us the poop on hypnotism; the plump and many-haired girl,
on the lost continent of Atlantis, speaks mildly,
sure of her actual eyes.
Farm boy, all pimples on a crooked face
   skeptical of itself, talks
      about the Battle of Chickamauga
         and other thangs, 'specially
            "Journal" Thomas, the Rock of Chickamauga.
Bloody. But dim bells ring the immediate hour
               and nobody has any questions anyway.

Next week we take up poetry. *Lawd, Lawd*!

SUMMER SCHOOL

Blood is just as new, but the roads it runs
are blocked and pot-holed; just for a summer, though,
almost any dog or jalopy revives when it goes back to school.

A beach of mirrors: the professor gazes on those who teach;
child-scolders grow into children and sit in rows.
Everyone sees not her image but someone else

in his own position, feeding the events he feeds,
dawdling through her role from another point of view.
Reflector, watching a drunk bend a road, voyeur,

voyageur, in a class all by myself, I face the void chair,
which, when my scholars leave, remains sitting,
having lost nothing in blood, and implacable.

AFTER PAPER GRADING

Whose words these are I think I know:
They are not by the student, though.
He will not see me stopping here
To watch his plagiarism grow.

My new assistant thinks it queer
To come on my sadistic leer
When it will take all week to make
These pounds of papers disappear.

She gives her hilly hair a shake
To ask if there is some mistake.
The only other sound's the sweep
Of deepening thought and dandruff flake.

The words are lovely, dark, and deep,
But not the student's – these will keep,
And I must number, like lost sheep,
Miles of prose before I sleep.

STRESS

The engineer who teaches here before me
Writes numbers on the board that, frankly, bore me.
Yet here and there amid the chalky mess
One word attaches my attention: *stress*.
Diagrams and equations pass me by,
Evade my all-too-little-seeing eye,
But when I spot that word we stress in common,
It makes our enterprises doubly human.

Of course, we traffic differently in pressures,
Intensities, stops, quickenings, and measures,
Especially those of the intellect
Appraising its designs, and I reflect,
As my eraser sweeps away his signs,
His is the stress of buildings, mine of lines.
He smiles as I arrive; defenses fall:
We have in common something, after all,
Something, that is, that doesn't hate a wall.

ORACLE

The hardest thing is not to talk nonsense.

Tell us the truth, they keep saying,
and all around you can hear the dishonesty.

Knowing for sure only small truths,
but paid to talk by the hour,

I grow hoarse, I grow hoarse.

Meetings

ASTONISHMENT

I was at a meeting: voices
failed to dissolve the walls,
air was nervous with structure,
nobody met, their hands
were grouped around some laugh,
the pediment in the library
mumbled, "*I can't get through,
I can't.*"

Feeling my skin grow old,
my neck tense, when the meeting
broke up in the usual loss
and rejected its people,
whose backs were walking away –
I came home and struck a lettuce
and laid open this india, this green
littoral.

DEFEAT AFTER DEFEAT

Anger at corruption –
not there, in Asia; here, in colleagues.
Beside me, in the council chair,
somehow materialized out of this secular life,
leers Pride the mushroom, unmistakable
in his dung beetle body.

If we had won, it might be me.
That thought, rolled up, pushed hard at,
will ease my indignation, in time chastise.
It can't restore. How, in my tipping house,
could it, to know, to acknowledge, that, faint, northeast,
that grubber humps me too?

MEETING TO FIND A CHAIRMAN

Folly, this talk: *Don't hurt me, gentlemen;*
leave bad enough alone; I would be king.
Under how to proceed, how to attack
uncertainty, what are we all defending?
What dream of beating are we keeping back?

Behind our folly the late afternoon,
beautiful, autumnal, drifts uncaucused, un-
decided. Oak leaves, aging, dry, and mum
as to successors, spin and scuff in the wind.
On what fool's errand have we hustlers come?

MEETING FATIGUE

No, Sir, when a man is tired of meetings he is tired of life.
— Samuel Johnson (?)

In the course of last week's
weekly meeting

I thought of the phrase,
the legend I crave

to be carved on my tombstone:
NO MORE MOTIONS

MOVE TO LIMIT DISCUSSION

At the first meeting
"I have an idea, too,"
cried a falling angel.

Dialogue's different –
*"What do you know that I
haven't got to yet?"*

To question the world
asks of us only that we see
how the world goes.

Sometimes the body's
so sick we feel it just ought
to start all over,

but even in headache
who would judge that course
as for him the right one?

It's all very well
to wave our drink and deplore
violence, plunder;

sooner or later
we have to hunt with the beast
that devours us.

At the last meeting
everyone's bright idea
will be out of order.

GARGOYLE

Liberal, sure, is pale,
but who may abide
the righteous radical?

In the name of truth
will stiffen every
half-decent institution,

in freedom's name
require absolute
convulsive conformity.

The reason of rage:
*play it my way, or else
I'll break up the damn game*.

Damn is always along
for those whose loyalty
is too loose, *damn them*

those who, innocent,
come by conviction
to a different view, *damn them*

those who notice
that even sons of bitches are
half-human, *damn them*

those who profess
doubt that any bright one
has all the answers, *damn them*

those who wonder whether
the best way to proceed
is to stop, *damn them*

those who are slow to put
the worst construction
on others' acts, *damn them*!

Damn, damn, damn, damn them!
Damn them all for not having
the guts to damn them!

Strange notion really
that intemperate hatred
fits you to govern

that the closed mind
will ever become, in another
setting, strong light

that the cup, Compassion,
tilts to relieve the thirst
only of our sort.

These moral centaurs –
guilt-ridden, self-righteous –
what a queer beast it is,

knowing uncertainty
as the dominant
tone of experience

yet sure that on every
issue that counts
their figuring is faultless.

The beast that John Calvin
in his walled city
caught, carved in adamant.

HOW TO STEP TWICE INTO THE SAME RIVER

I put the case perfectly, of course –
the unassailable position
argued irrefutably,
with just a few personal innuendoes tossed in
whose import could not be missed
nor, without loss of face, recognized.
The beautiful phrasing kept me whistling for days.

It happens all the time.
That is, it never happens.
What happens is, when the moment comes I muff it,
remain silent, choose the wrong word, cycle down
the unarguable path into a wet hedge.
Later – ah, later! –
the moment inches into a different perspective:
as I drive home, as I toss in bed,
a fairer scene begins to emerge,
climaxes take their place, sentences
round, ring into shape, periods
strengthen; opponents, abashed,
acknowledge the justness of my remarks,
the aptness of my figures. Struck,
they back down.

I put the case perfectly, of course.

Department Chair

ON BECOMING AN ADMINISTRATOR

At last
one with the universe

or at least
one with the University.

Words know: to succeed
means to go under.

JOB APPRAISAL

Managing now: a desk that papers climb,
each day some small injustice to be done,
some anger muffled for a higher good

these eyes gone crooked in the field discern,
this mouth goes tight at but articulates.
I wondered once how an astute ass, caught

in muddle, could face with a dry brow gibes and mockers.
Now it comes easy, General: what sustains
is that superior sense of task, the hedgerow

has to be taken, whatever galls, but, goddess
Irony, never desert me, make me laugh
when Utter Waste smirks through her interview.

JUNGLE

Now that my days are
altogether taken up with
problem-solving

it's only at night
that sometimes through dark sleep
I'm returned to myself,

to the fierce inner
Africa of being,
vulnerable, thoughtless,

as if, still, night by night, we were
hunted by the gorge's
shrieks and fangs

for food, not wisdom, not
love but that other
insatiable stalker.

Safe for another night,
no prowler having picked up
my scent or step,

I let in air, watch
the near and dreamless, clawless
powers take shape, the

non-carnivorous
shades of nerve and distance that today
will eat me.

CONSIDERATIONS

Considerations wake me in the night.
Everything, even sound, is quivering.
The city now, muffled in snow, abhors

evenly. Not a twig snaps, no car creeps.
All earth so dormant, how can history
resume in the morning, find it worth its while

to stir these absolute silences again, the new
paper of day superimpose upon this
patternless fall that rules everything equal?

Impossible. More impossible to abstain
from knowing it will happen, that day will
enlarge us, charm our power to suspend

further that genius for considerations
that charges even now the others' sleep
and lifts me here to where I softly curse their kind.

LOCAL DIGS

I

All alien, scratching in the dark at stones
scarred with some living speech, jabber to us.
What we most want a sense of, long to touch,

though any soul that age would think it odd
we'd need to ask. The ordinary life crumbles
around the pot that fires one hour of it

to baffle cautious clumsy foreigners:
ourselves wondering how the East Anglian scop
intoned, the cliffsite producers unearthing the

dance in front of the garbage, or the scholar from Japan
who remotely this morning through an interpreter groped
about my office for lost Fitzgerald's life.

II

And here am I, green in the water-city,
playing the two-glass game. *Stop*! I yell, *Stop*!
to the moment of the professor's bow, his gift, his

almost spilled coffee, my own quaking perception
of what's here in the room with us; and, later,
priming out of the poems I'm teaching this summer

the flow of life their grace gathered and hunches,
Begin, I whisper, *begin*, and to my sense
Keats from his well starts to send up that song.

Du bist so schön, some watcher in me says
in awe of this twin current, *Keep on*! *Repeat*!
till my halved strength tires of the swirling texts.

CHAIRMAN'S SONG

The seas of disagreement churn,
Anger and arrogance abound.
Let me, before they break, return
To scholar's, and to poet's, ground.

Deep inland, not to the salt edge
Where florid, wind-blown forms compete
For mastery of every ledge,
Mossed rock, sand spit, on which waves beat.

I have no captain in my soul
To stamp my image on the sea
And make its fathomed music roll
To my esthete's authority.

At times, it's true, the deck feels firm,
Sometimes the instruments enchant.
But every ship-stroll reaches term,
The seasick are not cured by cant.

And even in harbor, safe from violence,
Where this bark spends its privileged days,
One crew claque claims it owns those islands,
Prove-you're-a-God and *Grudge-me-no-praise*.

Another, better-natured, would
Steer with its toes and strut on wires,
Hoping only to make the good
Heart's fictions what the ship requires.

Instructive, but it can give no
Pleasure to hold loose strands of power
And watch the root resentments grow
Into a monstrous twisted flower

Watered by self-contempt, by pride
That heaves itself above small ferns,
Pressing its claims to be supplied
First with scarce air, and never learns

"*The modesty of nature*," that
Humanity we survive to teach
Somehow beneath the civil chat
Even on this uncivil beach.

The seas of disagreement churn,
Anger and arrogance abound.
Let me, before they break, return
To scholar's, and to poet's, ground.

ON LEAVING THE CHAIR

Now my days are all unnumbered,
Soon my nights will, unencumbered,
Fill with sleep's dark, deepening air,
All my guilts be put off there
Till I rise, untroubled moon,
Light as bubble or balloon,
Floating above wail or curse,
Through a dream of metered verse,
Cleared for life, and none the worse.

Old Companions

THREE OCCASIONAL POEMS

1. For Michael Dennis Browne

Michael, a lovely poem,
and in *The New Yorker*, what luck,
you fox, you assistant fox,

Or a new breed of hunter?
Watching patrolmen, foxes,
war in the Middle East,

you climb them into a poem
that never turns cruel.
Good fox Michael, good mirror,

before the cold committees
resume, let Snow Dog watch you
hang the new pelt in the house.

2. For Bill Rosendahl on His Retirement

Now that you're giving up the gown,
You'd think that Michael Dennis Browne
Would sing you to the eastern gate
With couplets that befit your state,
But to refrown his bardic brow
Michael is in England now
And in the absence of his flute
We tune this cruder substi-toot.

Sure, weaker Muses these days cast
Their pearls in meters of the past.
Only a light extravaganza
Fits any more a rhyming stanza.
Many a current poet's hand –
The more it moved, the less it scanned,
And Walt did more than Milton could
To make free verse the mark of good.

But for our present purposes,
When "English" on these premises
Has gathered to pay homage to
An honored colleague – Bill, that's you! –
Our hope is that a lighter verse,
Ragged, derivative, but terse,
Will, more than some grand vatic yell,
Yet sound sincere and suitable.

We use it, then, this diapason,
To mark the mood of this occasion:
Festive, restrained, a trifle sad,
As colleague, mentor, husband, dad,
Teacher, chairman, honest friend,
Strong to advise or to commend,
Good academic citizen,
Achieves his threescore years and ten.

Northwestern tried to discipline ya.
From there you went to West Virginia
Before you added to your quota
Another Northwest: Minnesota.
But, in between, a different hat
Was yours to wear with honor at
That other campus (known for truth?):
Remote and booster-backed Duluth.
There in the steep and frigid air
You spent years as department chair.

Through all this time you've known the blighting
Pleasures and pains of student writing.
Many a morning, work and care
Have met you in the chairman's chair.
Many an hour, more's the pity,
You've passed in meeting or committee,
Observed, as sun gave place to sun,
How much that's done is soon undone.
Before you, as you've neared this day,
You've seen some younger powers play
And kept, through all the revolutions,
Humor, perspective, no illusions.

From '49 to '84,
Precipitous Superior's shore
To the Twin Cities' double campus,
You've watched our vogues and fashions stamp us:
Formalist, historical,
Marxist, phenomenological,
Symbolist, psychoanalytical,
New- and post-New and hyper-critical,
Intertextual, deconstructible,
Lacanian, feminist, ineluctable.
We've learned to watch, cross-disciplined,
Fastidious, fractious, and thin-skinned.

While all these tempests have been brewing,
You've stayed serene and kept on doing.
The Nestor of our warlike clan,
Strong in council, tempered man,
Close reader of the human page,
The green with youth or dulled with age,
Through all our shrillness, rage, invective,
You've kept your balance and perspective.

Retiring? Well, we count on you
To teach another class or two
And celebrate, with cheese and sherry,
Sinclair Lewis's centenary.
But all such forms of stimulation
Require the tools of contemplation.
To think and exercise their wit
All chairmen need a place to sit.

We picture you in spring and later
Reading in Wordsworth, Keats, and Pater,
Reading for pleasure, with cool drink,
Proust or Mann or Maeterlinck.
We see you sitting on the green
With this thick CUSHION in between
You and the bug-beleaguered grass
But not preparing for a class.
But if you're not content with that,
A REDWOOD CHAIR comes with the mat.
A seat out in the open air:
That's the best department chair.
Enjoy long hours of repose
With gripping novels and loose clothes,
And think of us as we of you,

Affectionately,

All the crew

3. A Volley for Eric, at Fifty

It's natural but not so nifty
That one should feel less fit at fifty,
Should count the clock and climb the walls,
And play with blemished (tennis) balls.
It hardly matters if you swerve
On smashes or if every serve
Betrays a chronic loss of nerve.
What's more important is the style
With which, and an engaging smile,
You cover up your ebbing guile.
Your old companions at the net
Won't notice how your knees forget,
When the low deep drives come, to bend,
How long the back pain takes to mend,
Or if in forecourt, poised to crush
A meager lob, and make us blush,
You raise your racquet to the weather
And miss the missile altogether.
These things will happen more and more –
Take it from one who's gone before.
From now on every muff and miss
We'll treat as a parenthesis.
And knowing that you can't not do them,
We'll just not call attention to them.
What else, in fact, are we to do?
Remember we're all aging, too.

POKER

Seven round men ·
around a table toss
colored chips to the center

hanging their wealth as it
were on these deaf defanged
royal rank-watchers.

Although the democratic
high-low expresses
a fitting rebuke

to mere naked power
however suited,
it still rewards the fine.

Who would have searched
under this round lamplight for
true meritocracy?

Dealer's choice: that means
changing the frames so the
novels can write themselves

to which, between beers,
hot plates, salads, French bread,
and trips to the pissoir,

we attend diligently,
caught up in this Matter,
this Count-Country

where three deuces justly
prevail over two kings
but a mob's worthless.

The tone must be kept:
five souls of more than a
common complexion

out-earn a ragtail
higgledy-piggledy
sequence of yes-persons

but yield in turn
to the rhythmic counterpoint
of threeness and twoness.

To the improbable
all-of-a-kind even
these highnesses bow

but nothing out-argues
five cards committed
to passion *and* order,

unless, of course, the state
has been abandoned
wholly to wildnesses.

Even a devoted anarchist
nevertheless
sees a point in rules:

if weather won't,
at least some posts have to
keep being predictable,

for numbers are relative
and seven round men
wittingly human

who monthly perform this
celebration of
circular excellence.

MEMENTO

He's sat on my desk for years,
that six-inch clown, wound down, minus his hat.
Black coat, blue cufflinks, red nose, red cravat.
They married us with beers,

rude speeches, cracks, bad verse
when I came north a dozen years ago
to where, through every winter's thickening snow,
while the fouled land's grown worse,

under his closed white eyes
my own life's craft, subtler but still grotesque,
made with the tided bed and fervent desk
its fateful compromise.

This cheap and comic Sven,
look, if I turned the lever in his back,
would even now whirr, stir his feet, and clack
to time my falls again.

THE NEW MODELS

At every turn I've checked the road ahead:
      kid, I watched some older kid;
as older kid, copied the carbon sage
      cocky, complete, twenty, sweaty,
      but when I came to be his age
admired the maturity of thirty.

At thirty I knew envy for the tan
      professional, the tuned-up man
aware at all speeds, poised, perfected, wise.
      Now I am there where no more turns
      show models to my still shifting eyes.
The figures that my vision now discerns

up there, ahead, have all gone horribly wrong,
      sagged blind into the ditches, sprung
dangerous leaks, or simply run down and sit
      in stalled machines and drily watch
      me, young comers wreathed in sweat,
or some whole kid our accident can't touch.

SAMLA, 1967*

A carful of questions, jokes, gripes, witty asides,
tossed up for two hundred miles to Atlanta.
One, "highly articulate," sprinkles his syntax with curse words;
one sulks with a laugh; one leaves his glasses behind
                    at a roadside cafe.

The weather is blue, Atlanta jammed, we collect
our hotels and dismiss our car. At lunch
John Tinkler appears, invites, dematerializes.
And then old faces, older this year, begin
                    their smiling, bare-child tramp

across my tearing page. The papers are all too long,
the paperers too self-pleased. Why is everyone grinning?
Crazed by the yellow light that crisps our faces,
revulsion like a gangster, fatigue like a film
                    gun us all down.

Or so it seems to me who abscond for a nap
in a poisonous mood and wake wary but clear.
Evening cools, disperses veils and voices.
Under smoked scotch the pieces for a while are radiant
                    and just where I put them.

But the morning light, highly articulate, smiles
its void at our crowded, questioning eyes. Atlanta,
powered by sleep, cashes our next year's handshakes.
Schooled, in the sludge of noon we scatter home
                    to pick up fogged-up lives and glasses.

*SAMLA is the South Atlantic Modern Language Association, which, in the years I
taught at the University of Tennessee (Knoxville), used to hold its annual fall meetings
every other year in Atlanta.

CONVENTION STROLL, 1991

Cold wind in Vancouver,
but out to get free of the word-wind
for an hour's walk,

mapless, in quest of views,
I wander past the glass and concrete blocks,
drift into a museum,

but no, it isn't art I want, not
anything formed to formulate.
Out of thought, I rush out, scarred,

into the gnashing wind again,
up likely streets, down wrong ones, till, yes, there –
mountains and sea at the end of one,

follow it till it flares
into a bay – beyond, I suppose: Victoria.
I fit it into my saved similar

pictures – Swiss lakes, mountain-marged –
but this is here, new, not now in my grasp,
utterly unfamiliar, so I keep it

carefully not yet mine, an uncarved coast,
developing, as these embankment piles, scaffolding, scholars
plot to destroy it from the other end.

AUCTOR MAGNUS, AUCTOR MORTUUS

This campus is dead from the biceps up.
Its every athlete is a famous man,
like Jesus, General Lee, and Coach Rupp.

Hail to the champion baller, the campus queen.
May all their progeny have strength and grace
to make a hit, never to make a scene,

because, God knows, brute chest or pretty face,
they'll never here caress it out of books.
We asked a famous novelist to this place

who only had a mind and not good looks.
The cheerleaders didn't show up. The hall, though brighter
than the Orange Bowl, still lacked a lot in *lux*.

The bodies stayed away in drifts, liter-
ary scholars notably deeply. Bitter.
The only good writer is a dead writer.

TO A VISITING SCHOLAR, IN DEFENSE
OF THE PROVINCES

You'd have us feel, nothing in this Siberian
backwater, in this culture, can be first-rate,
a flat American anti-ironic pall
corrupts the scholar and the writer. True.
True, but we must make do with what we have,
with what we are, flat, American, wanting
your European depth. We carry on
something, here in the shallows, that won't surprise
visiting breakers thrown our way by the sea
but still may nourish, crawling up the exhausted
beach, some gross, awkward sea-cow charged with life.

LITERARY SCHOLARS

Captured, young,
by the hideous witch
whom we of course adore,
we discover by trial
only one release:

minute attention
to the hem of her skirt,
analysis, microscopic,
of the skin-wrinkles
in the sockets of her eyes.

That golden hair,
the bite into blood,
moon through tough trees on snow,
waves of sea-words,
are by this engine

slowed to muck.
Out in the street
with the safe little trees,
Mm, which is the brownstone
where one wooed Circe?

LIT'RY MEMOIR

The famous names drip-drop across the page
and make at last a puddle of the dead –
mocking the weak great writers of the age,
plugging the second-rate, the great unread.
Forty years later, from a lowered stage:
"One bright December morning Someone said . . ."

Urbanity? Here literature's become
meager, trivial, unreflective, small,
its refuse Someone's banquet, its least crumb
the instrument of Someone Else's fall.
I'd rather write in darkness, be struck dumb
than jostle in that damp, diminished hall.

SCRATCH SHEET

> *Not, I think, a mind of the first force.*
> – One leading critic, of another, in conversation

Of the fourteenth, perhaps. From far behind,
The sixty-second or the eighty-fifth,
I watch the big cheeks waddle down the course –
Not, I think, arses of the first horse.

IDEAL TISSUES

The enervation of burning odours, the
baptismal whiteness of women, light,
ideal tissues, eyes strangely dark with kohl.
– George Moore, *Confessions of a Young Man*

The best kind – no mistakes, no strain, no blood,
not in time, but still tissues: so one could
make thoughts, not women, out of wine, not wood.

Yet something will elude the mind: not love –
near any touch will help that hermit live –
but the commonplace chapel of demand, and give

(which pure George Moore had scant experience of).

MUMMY

Lover, courtier, churchman, "Frequenter
of Plays," "great Visitor of Ladies," wit,
John Donne, I will not make you into what
I would be if I had been you. I've read a Life
that treats your facts. Your poems long ago
dissolved them, as we slough selves. Buried alive
in sundry Pauline business, you'd not believe
what a huge acne'd Honors English crew
even this late, on touch, you turn into.

TAKING SOME LIBERTIES WITH JENNIE

Lester was gone, but at least she had Vesta.
— Dreiser, *Jennie Gerhardt*

Lester was gone, but at least she had Vesta.
Vesta was here, she insisted, to test her.
Lester was gone and had not even missed her,
Though when he had left he had hastily kissed her,
      Fussed her and mussed her,
      Really nonplussed her,
      Almost undressed her.
Now Lester was gone, but at least she had Vesta.

But the luster of Lester diminished the faster
As the vista of talents of Vesta grew vaster.
At Easter no pastoral bastard was chaster.
Alas to relate, when curst autumn caressed her,
      She stiffened and wasted,
      Fierce typhoid oppressed her,
      Soon Jennie had lost her,
And now her nest boasted no Lester nor Vesta.

Had Dreiser been wiser, he might just have cast her
With clusters of hucksters, boisterous boosters,
Mobsters, imposters, transvestites who'd vexed her
And itched to accost her unclasped in a cloister
      And would have enticed her,
      Engrossed her, seduced her
      (For Lust was their master).
That might have been monstrous, distasteful, but zestful.

But Dreiser, obsessed with a lesser disaster,
Must have her reduced at all costs – not one sister,
Not Lester, not Vesta, no least friend had lasted.
For Jennie, estranged, a destiny drastic
     And hostile, Midwestern:
     Not pistol and holster
     But caustic and distance
And solitude, plastic, unflustered but wistful.

Envoi

O Theodore, awed in your rich little slum
At how far you and Jennie and Carrie have come,
Your fables compel, you've a feel for sex woes,
If only, old buck, you had learned to write prose.
Where anyone else would have named the girl Sue
Or Phyllis or Fanny or Margaret, you,
Deaf to all tone, call the little girl Vesta,
Deaf to all sound, call the next lover Lester.
Theodore, Theodore, deaf to your toes,
What bone in your body composed your bad prose?

GUIDE TO ANCIENT GREECE

In Athens, on the thoughtful stones,
    Philosophy was born.
In Arcady, young bodies danced,
    Lithe nymph with lusty faun.
Out at sea Poseidon's wrath
    Chasmed the level lawn.
On Lesbos, under an olive tree,
    Rosy fingered Dawn.

FIGURES

Woke with an idea for a story – two old
scholars, both retired, one still in bondage,
reading together some obscure epic written
in some improbable language, the *Davidssaga*
(could there be such an opus?), the younger crusty,

resentful, poor, seventy, distinguished, obliged to
teach still after retirement, but at a more modest
school, where B, less notable but of a somewhat
placider mind, seventy-five, years into his
superannuation, out of courtesy becomes

the only pupil to sign up for the course
in a close reading of the minor poem.
They spar a bit: *"I don't want to impose,"*
"No imposition at all, quite the reverse,
so seasoned an ephebe" – and they settle

to read the poem twice a week in the office of A.
There I see them, B jogging along,
forbidden his pipe now, jaunty wit, alert,
improving his mind here at the slip of life,
getting to what's of moment – those lapsed lines,

the edge between grass and flower bed, evening whiskey,
air yet breathworthy, neighborhood misadventures
from last week, nothing further back but style:
"Isn't that the same figure Milton uses . . .?" And even
A, who is reputed to love his work

and doesn't, used to, begins again to, at least to
respond to Beetleman's warmth and shine. A's skills
seem princely next to poor Broderick's merely intelligent
guesswork, uninformed, undisciplined
by knowledge of the genealogy of cognate forms,

the magnetic field of philological discourse.
Why is it, then, that Arneson feels awakened
by his old, innocent pupil, more than by
years of youngsters, some as yare as you'd wish,
who'd kept the codes in better order, and even with

randomer lives, distractions, came to the work
cleared for discovery, compulsive pens, memories, notebooks
bending to this day's tesseral enigma –
copy it, grasp it! – straining to tease a pattern
from chance bits coiling in those brimming minds

unfixed by form yet, only the form of fire,
while Brighthurst brings to his text a mastery
that drenches even his mild linguistic insights?
I have squandered my life on the young, Angvik thinks
in despair, as they pick their way through the last fragment,

where, amid coughs and wheezes, the boy David,
whom this long labor has surprised emerging
from his late Northern shelf, stands, stretches, yawns,
grins at their tent of words and slings at it
an average stone –
                    as sleep slung them at me.

FACULTY REPORT

In this year Professor Ethelbert Kleinkin published
nothing, he was translated, an uncommon fever
seized him. On summer evenings, still within spearshot

of shouts along the embankment, he began to learn.
This is different, he thought. After that the forms
of anxiety ever active within him altered

their tenure, or so it seemed to selected colleagues.
His seminar grew unruly. It met nights
in meadows to count moonlight. After one brush

with actual police, he gave up receiving
students entirely. "*What I know*," he said cunningly,
"*is of a different order from the curriculum*,"

and blew out the candle. Wellington Winter, his
curmudgeonly ally, he roundly suspected of
shilly-shallying and said so. Toward the end he declined

even to sit with committees, and the dean, quite in tears,
offered to let him teach a whole new language.
He became a retention case, finally the vice-president

went, the one for Academic Affairs.
Useless. "*I am not*," Kleinkin told him through a side window, "*now
nor have I ever been an academic*

affair." Predictably, his student credit hours
dwindled. Once or twice remarked in the town
radiant with some unprofessional awareness,

he was heard to construe imagery. When, in late spring,
his scribble came, "*Yes, I'm signed up for the Great Course yonder*,"
someone in Budget thought to delete his line.

DOSSIER

My primary professional objective is to pursue
a career in college teaching. I wish to become
a full professor. Short-termwise my goal

is to hopefully overcome my stylistic hang-ups
and become imbued with the metaphysical poets.
Recently I have surprised in myself an affinity

for unrhymed verse, which I mean to further indulge
by taking a long close look at Sylvia Plath
in the context of gender. If things go according to plan,

my thesis will be published by the Oxford Press.
Questions 2 and 16 I consider degrading, otherwise
your curriculum meets my present needs. Please send fellowship.

VITA

The cry of the unsung,
*"If I live long enough,
someone will notice,"*

modulates into
*"Should the world come to nothing,
it wasn't my fault."*

Just Yard

THE DISEMBOWELERS

Righteous Anger,
Left-handed Irony –
which will get to do us in?

THE ENEMY

Hatred, beginning as tiny as any power
        in the world-person,
kills or disqualifies some, but may learn to gather,
        to mass, organize.
When that occurs, whatever the doctrine, the stated
        goal, whether freedom,
fellowship, sanity, health, peace, trust, even love,
        that man is my enemy.

Not to be killed but resisted, not to be hated,
        the object of rage,
but worked against with all lines, as one strains against brutal
        weather or ignorance,
forced back, hand-hold by hand-hold, down fear and cliff-face,
        made to give ground
at least half back to the clearing, where life without irony
        warms into blossom.

And when in myself, too, even in me the enemy
        inflates and surfaces,
he must meet hard rock. When in a thousand disguises,
        through fatigue and lust,
that desperate Fascist native in all but a few of us
        starts scolding and scourging,
oppose, to the death station your average frame
        in the human doorway.

THERE'S A LESSON HERE SOMEWHERE

> Harvard University's president, Nathan Pusey, left a Senate
> hearing room in Washington, D.C., in a huff after he was
> not called to testify as scheduled about student disorders on
> his campus. "I consider this a great indignity," Pusey said.
> "I got up at 4:30 this morning to come all the way down
> here. I cannot be here tomorrow. I have a commitment."
>
> – News item, 1969

The class of men that never stand in line,
no one keeps waiting.

How does it feel to be treated once in your life like
a minor oyster?

Indignity, discourtesy, frustration, boredom? Hey, that's
what it's all about, man.

Waiting, ignored, powerless – like undressed in
the doctor's office –

dealt with as No-name by the arms of state,
in the death-file if needed,

each man alone at the passionless center of immense
organization

so that no street, no lamplight, no public message, no whip points
direction or prospect.

And now by the millions they are ready to rise in a huff, saying,
I have an appointment.

What do you offer them, you so acutely conscious
of yourself and Harvard?

At Harvard, does no one ever have to wait to rap with
Trustee or President?

You will be subjected to deeper indignities
by an earthier senate.

Vietnam Tunes

1. SOUTHERN CHARM, USA

You think it clever to claim the South
won that grand war it might have won,
that what was done was in fact not done.

No imagery of gaping mouth,
red-spattered boots, arrests your laughter
all these maimed generations after.

Your mischievous remarks assert
a myth of loss, the wish to hurt.
The epic is far-off and cute.

So if soiled images arise
of new chivalric enterprise,
laugh, and bid the soldiers shoot.

2. STATE DEPARTMENT SPOKESMAN

He smiles and lisps; on his bald head –
he's cut himself – not quite dried blood.
"War ith unpleathant," he lisps and smiles.

"When I wath in Thaigon" – sincere,
affected, phony, all his fear
rolled up in manner, false by miles.

His logic childish, full of holes,
his lips *"contherned"* at killing souls,
agreeable, hopeless to move.

Sucking the mammoth teat of State,
has found asylum, a place to sit
and lisp of reasonable love.

3. OLD GLORY

Civilians everywhere! How can a bomb
Distinguish Cong and peasant in Vietnam?

What if we slaughter humans in a hutch?
It isn't practical to care too much.

What if we scorch the trees and scald the rice?
In war to be too virtuous is a vice.

Kill everything that moves: it may be man,
So kill it – and then count it if you can.

*   *   *   *

We have a dream: that all men shall be brothers,
Except the poor, the Commies, and some others.

Nations shall learn, however various,
To live, though less enlightened, just like us.

Then man may sell to man in any street
And, as in Paradise, be free to cheat.

We find this vision so intense, so thrilling,
So holy, it will sanctify any killing.

*   *   *   *

For every home broken by TNT,
We promise freedom under Marshall Ky.

For every colored kid burned with napalm,
We promise freedom like in Alabam.

For all this violence dropped, driven, hurled,
We proffer membership in the free world,

A seat next some bright democratic star
Like Franco, Onganìa, Salazar.

*   *   *   *

The general sticking pins into a map:
"One escalation ought to wrap it up."

The Secretary, with his sleight-of-hand,
His real half-million soldiers on the land:

"China's the one! China makes all the trouble!"
And blows away reality like a bubble.

The President, admiring his jaw:
"Why, that's the ugliest thang I ever saw."

4. CHORUSES FROM AN ESCALATOR

Chorus of Voices (from below):
   The law of escalation is not a law for the meek:
   Whatever goes up goes up and up, whatever comes down is weak.
   We prove that we have mettle, they prove that they've got grit,
   And we proudly show the results to the world, if there's anything left
                                                                    of it.

General:
   I hate to bomb a village, though I do it very well.
   I pray sometimes for peace, as I'm convinced that war is hell.
   But I've never been promoted for suggesting we withdraw.
   The law of escalation is a very human law.

Chorus of Solid Citizens:
   The President alone has all the facts and must decide.
   If he says we must fight, then we must fight with faith and pride,
   To save mankind from being told just what to think and feel.
   The law of escalation has great popular appeal.

President:
   We must honor our commitments, we must push aggression back,
   Prop up all friendly governments, just, unjust, white or black.
   We've got to show the Commies that they can't push us around.
   The law of escalation has a very manly sound.

Secretary of State:
   For if we waver, one by one the states of Asia fall,
   Forever irrecoverable, condemned beyond recall.
   We'd rather kill them off at once, and therefore we oppose
   The law of escalation to the law of dominoes.

Vice President:
   Yes, under the godless Communists life is a different thing.
   No one makes love or laughs out loud, no one may wash or sing.
   All their leaders are evil, we elect only upright men.
   The law of escalation will make everyone good again.

The Secretary of Defense (30 years later):
    I knew the war was futile, but I couldn't say so with tact.
    To tell the truth would be awkward, to resign a disloyal act.
    Better three million peasants burn on a backward subcontinent
    Than one of the best and brightest should embarrass his President.

Republicans:
    We've kind thoughts for a war that can't be won by a Democrat.
Viet Cong and Ho Chi Minh:
    We'll wait a year or a century; we have nothing to do but that.
    Asia will come to hate the tyrant less than the meddling fool.
All: The law of escalation is the opposition's tool.

Mao and Chou:
    We have comrades in Tirana, we have conquered far Tibet,
    We have come to love the bomb, we have our family quarrels, yet
    When it comes to ways of burying – the riot, the knife, the knot –
    The law of escalation is our favorite of the lot.

Oswald, Ruby, Speck, Whitman, Sirhan, Ray, et al.:
    When Mommy slaps you in the teeth, when Daddy kicks you in the
                                            head,
    Just wait awhile, then buy a gun and shoot some people dead.
Black Militants and White Vigilantes:
    Fight aggression with aggression; what is murder but self-defense?
All: The law of escalation serves the god of violence.

Chorus of Leaders, Parties, Peoples, Particles (as they vanish, above):
    The law of escalation is not a law for the meek:
    Whatever goes up goes up and up, whatever comes down is weak.
    We prove that we have mettle, they prove that they've got grit,
    And we show the proud results to the world – or whatever's left of it.

5. PINKVILLE

> My Lai was one of nine hamlets . . . clustered near
> the village of Songmy . . . .The men of Company C
> called the area "Pinkville" . . .
>   – *Life*, December 5, 1969

The homegrown names won't do, they accuse
in a mirror dialect – *my song, me lie*.
What is a lie, a song, or a slang name
but conversion, translation, what is massacre but
another strategy to change *them* into *us*?

Pinkville, of course: politics given color,
our *own, our* town, where black and white (as a team!)
turn against life, kill women, kids,
cows, pigs, rice, houses, everything that moves.
A soldier in a field runs down a duck.

Well, it was a crazy morning there
defending freedom: then freedom is
to kill? At least one man said "*No*," and one
preferred maiming his foot to murdering people.
But no one opposed, the cameraman kept clicking . . .*

I can still hear the machine guns playing my song.
Wires are helping me lie: *it was only there,
it will never happen again*. No, not to them.
In Pinkville, with good reason, we disdain,
lovers of peace, even to find the graves.

---

*But someone did oppose, as I learned from a newspaper thirty years
later. From his Army helicopter Warrant Officer Hugh Thompson saw
what was going on, landed his plane, and with his two men prevented
further slaughter at gunpoint.*

VILLANELLE, 1970

I wake in the small hours, warm with outrage,
outrage and horror at the year's injustice –
Biafra, My Lai, Prague, Judge Julius Hoffman.

Cold asleep, drowned in everybody's darkness,
from dreams of burned-out villages and courtrooms
I wake in the small hours, warm with outrage.

The ignorant resume their play of wisdom,
the wars go on, the massacres, busts, purges,
Biafra, My Lai, Prague, Judge Julius Hoffman.

What can help, what direct word, what sure action?
The night exhausts me with imagined programs.
I wake in the small hours, warm with outrage.

And everywhere good men despair of goodness,
die of diseases with such names as Athens,
Biafra, My Lai, Prague, Judge Julius Hoffman.

What can I do but string names and remember,
but call out names and evil, never coldly?
I wake in the small hours, warm with outrage:
Biafra, My Lai, Prague, Judge Julius Hoffman.

THE MUSIC BOX, OR PLAY IT AGAIN, HARRY

December, 1972

When Roosevelt died, I heard it
among the jeeps and trucks
at breakfast in Vacha,
trim little town in Thüringen.

German planes in the night
had shot it up a bit,
scared out of his texts
our religious nut, who cowered

and curled up small as he could,
sweating, in the interior hallway.
They'd cleared for our couple of squads
a doctor's middle-class household

whose family, judging from photos,
was more or less Nazi. One got
a pretty fair sense of their layers,
flipping through family things,

old albums, postcards, schoolbooks,
the curios crowning the mantel
and dressers, all to be whisked now,
loot, into duffel bags,

with violins, lace embroidery,
typewriters, rifles, Turkish
cigarettes, porcelain, pots –
"*Liberate everything portable!*"

Did we stay two nights at Vacha?
I dimly recall a kind of
Sunday walk among greenhouses –
or was that in Steinheid or Suhl?

In the morning, on top of dried eggs,
we heard about Roosevelt's headache
and felt historic: Truman
assumed the Presidency

there in the makeshift motor pool
on the edge of Vacha.
A few days into his tenure
I am sitting in a den-like room

pointing a gun at a man
whom I intend to shoot
if he moves suddenly,
instead we talk French,

our twenty words or so,
we discuss the war, he asks
who will be President now,
Truman, I say, he laughs.

Towns later, on Truman's birthday,
the war blew out like a cake,
so we got to sleep on the ground again.
Germany, scattered and gathered

within me, glows this week
while Truman dies in the newspapers.
I still have a music box
that I freed from the doctor's flat,

knowing it wouldn't stay long
if I set it back down, and a text
of Catullus, old cohort, I've lately
surprised myself skimming again.

OUR MYTH

Kill joy, kill time, kill the rest of the bottle –
it's a fine day, fine country for killing.

A hundred heroes good at the gun, our gun,
the kindly man who kills for their own good,

the rough hombre, driven by luck or plot
into a corner, comes out six-guns blazing

while the others in the dream always miss
or it's just a flesh wound or the flawed buddy gets it

for whom there was no place in the good town after.
Someone had to die. Too bad it had to be him.

Grave in the desert, skewed cross over stones
pacify dead Joe Guilt, fucking becomes

the next order of business, all the pollution
nailed, and half a life still to be killed.

ON EVOLUTION

Wishing for purpose, we discover at last our long aimlessness,
the accidental propriety of the big brain
and the futility of early success.
For the long tail turns out to be too handy,
the chimpanzee's agility too sufficient,
the red-butted baboon too adept at attack in concert.
It is always the neurotic, the left-back one who, losing his trees
and scanning his fear with his throat, invents something stupid like a word.

Later, with infinite hands, I reach out and touch
the sickening air at Hiroshima.
Liberal, I warm with my fingers
injustice, I cradle in my arms international pain. Sympathy,
the perspective of other, hypothesis, teach me again
child's rage, child's helplessness, in the time before words.
I have most need of blessing – and the next step.

JUSTICE

I worked for the SP once as a yard clerk
and learned the lingo, on the graveyard shift
saw the immense, dead silent boxcars drift
down tracks whose trembling warned me through the dark.

Old Irishmen ruled there, still vest-attired,
proud of their worn suits and seniority,
and one plump failed intellectual, Ted Hugé,
they ridiculed, took for a company spy, and fired.

Injustice everywhere! yet what recurs,
years later, stronger than his predicament,
is the burring night music of those monsters
powering down the rails – a dead event

impersonal, remorseless, harrowing, maternal, weird.
Ages older, I know as I couldn't then,
when I grew indignant for Ted against those gray men,
what seniority is worth in the just yard.

Classical Failings

Structured Shore

AQUARIUM

The old fish fiddle with their fins and glide.
As if I had their water in my eyes,
      My body skates from side to side
Before the glass square that defines their motion,
      And wonders how they moralize
The evened edges of their narrowed ocean.

What rich escapes, through black walls greenly weeded,
From pirate shark, flounder, or captain squid,
      Must plank the brain no longer needed!
Nights – to give plausibility, even ground,
      To what in fluider days they did –
They flee in one-eyed angles round and round.

Once the sly currents of the Gulf flowed cool
And fanned their gills with luminous information;
      The wit of drains in a heated pool
Alone selects them now. All's bright and blank
      In the captive phase of evolution.
Ecology is different in a tank.

Here, in asparagus light, schooled to the turns,
The management providing every dish,
      They drill their fins around the ferns
And take a gurgling pleasure in the glare.
      They know: the style, it is the fish.
Their side of the glass, water is everywhere.

ZOO

At loose ends, jittery, dejected, jarred,
Wishing direction, dour, nothing to do,
Escaped without resource, all prospects barred,
I took my bare perceptions to the zoo.
Brushed by a wind that aired their cages too,
I watched the wondrous animals behave
In habitats unnatural and new.
I saw the lion lumber from his cave
As if his strength were real and his observers brave.

The baggy hippo pondered in a pool;
A tiger steered his muscles in the sun;
The thick gorilla chomped his golden stool;
On a wide stone, close ranked, ton hunched to ton,
Three elephants lifted their trunks in fun
To pour a screech in one another's ears.
This side of pitfall, safe from spear and gun,
Baffled no more by elemental fears,
They wrinkle in the smog and yawn away the years.

Do they, with rudimentary nostalgia,
Regret the violence of veldt and grove?
Here by the sea they suffer from neuralgia,
Bumps in the skin, sick eyes, and boring love.
Each with his kind abstracted, bribed to move
Among the odors of old enemies,
How do they pacify the memory of
That other jungle's jousts and victories,
Where passions prowled veins more tumultuous than these?

Now in their specialized apartment blocks
The idle inmates learn the art of man.
If bears, they scoop up peanuts from the rocks
Or sit, toes out, and catch them as they can.
The guarded deer, who when approached once ran,
Now lick their supper from a youngster's palm.
How different from the ground where life began,
This littered Eden, and the offered arm
Their sniffs find friendly and their feeding habits charm.

Down other walks I pass the burdened yak,
The acrobatic gibbon and his wail,
The nervous, bearded lion-tailed macaque,
The blinking monkey, whose returning tail
Clasps like an afterthought the columned jail
His cousins fixed here to contain his rage
And pose his fancy talents till they fail.
Flushed with success, flamed by this mammoth cage,
I wish them vehement against their vassalage.

Ridiculous! Haired, natural, bizarre,
They do not tremble yet with two-times-two,
Nor wonder as they peer past moat and bar
What any child might ask: *Then who is who?*
Am I a baby monster just like you?
While the great questions quicken and exhaust,
They only formulate the food in view.
What have our various confinements cost?
They cannot place themselves, but I alone am lost.

MUSEUM

I

The tourists quicken with a noisy awe,
Sniff values as their guides sweep them along
The coffered staircase and the marble floor
Where muscular, nude, half-world Hebrews throng
In Roman courtyards and in Bacchic song,
In Spanish beards or an Italian copse.
I feel baroque myself but lack a gong.
With so much flesh, though, interest never drops.
Astonished at the Velazquez room, everyone stops.

In keeping with their gift for fantasy,
Americans are guided to the Bosch.
A sort of English in a sort of plea
Tells how to take him and warns not to touch.
"Look, Mabel, waterskis!" The witty bunch
Crowd the vision, make it a group joke.
"Let's leave the Goya until after lunch."
"Ralph said something so clever àpropos of Van Dyck:
'I don't know much about art but I know what not to dislike'."

Yet something gets through, like grass through concrete,
Insights hungering upward through the cracks
In the paved skull: *"Now why would a man do that,*
Care about catching that cast of the hand, those looks
Leering at Christ, care that much if he makes
The folds of the robes just right, and all those cubes
Narrowing in the distance like train tracks?
I couldn't care less – but, boy, look at those boobs:
It's amazing what they squeeze out of those goddamn tubes!"

So, living next to still and final forms,
The season's chaff glean the enduring wheat,
Hurrying down the stairs to other storms,
Past the experienced postcards, through stiff heat,
To the intense, white, momentary street,
Stone that turns to stone while persons pass
From life to life on surely failing feet.
Only the painter's peering stirs the grass,
Makes pause of movement, and of murdering water, glass.

II

The great museum at Barcelona comes to mind:
The moving colors and the poignant scenes.
How awkwardly the stilted figures stand,
How unnaturally the mother leans,
Scowling her gracious love from golden screens.
As Isaac waits for death among the lambs,
He has no look to question what it means.
Frescoes are still iconic diagrams,
Coloring cases of the cosmic apothegms.

On loggias of medieval courts
Ignorance, evil lust for the death of Christ.
His skin is slitted. Gouts of blood like warts
Spill from the nails. Now colors of the West
Begin to flow the robes and light the blest
Into a world of differing depths and powers.
Quiet insight yields to epic zest.
Realms of near flesh command the distant towers.
The people become real, and the perspective ours.

And yet not altogether so. The views
Seem too much chosen to light up the art.
The problem-solver drops his prudent clues,
Which make us watch our lives, now worn apart.
Technology is blooded like the heart.
Richer but less at one, we all aspire,
After this stumbling, stimulating start,
To know for certain and be free to err,
Not to be simpler but to live as if we were.

Picture and moment clatter in the dark
Of these considerations. Who would guess
That a naive, unskeptical age could work
Its wobbles forward, widen its distress
To wail for the most opulent loneliness
Of an unimagined, kingless, remote domain?
How did we come to be thrown together like this –
Tempi, tempera, mores, boobs, old Spain –
All foreign to one another, all figured in paint and pain?

It's that a museum isn't only what's on the walls,
It's people taking in what is still around,
What still endows them, what from breath still falls
Before its formulations reach the ground.
Maybe the idea of a museum, after all, is sound.
So I think as the crowd, El-Greco-wise,
Given art's patient power to astound,
Resume their revels with augmented eyes.
I look some more at boiling martyrs and cracked skies.

TOURING

Gray eminence, that purrs above the town,
Madonna-of-the-postcards, through whose glass
The broken light of heaven comes mended down
And whose black, tapered worshippers yet press
To catch the vacant visions as they pass,
Sustain us, reverent in our modern way,
Who sort out styles and guidebooks during Mass.
Indulge our energetic naiveté
And light our bank of flames from your obscurity.

Voyaging, voyaging . . . Imperious
As lust, this rage for travel shakes us, scares.
We rummage through this Europe like a house,
Seeking images misplaced somewhere upstairs,
Establishing our rights as missing heirs
To touch the woodwork in the attic, know
Whose unseamed skin these gold curved scimitars
Break, to which mured church ancient murderers flow,
Their colored clothes in keeping, their abstractions slow.

We stroll at large among their speaking tombs
As if by free election. Some lash drives
The touring spirit to inspect these rooms,
To reawaken rigid kings and wives
And pose them in the mirror of ourselves;
Acknowledging their purer walls and towers,
To ask their blessing on our better lives,
Our fuller vision, our more published powers,
To lift the cloth between their innerness and ours.

The green, august, and coded countryside,
Whose script once urged concession or attack,
Today, by noise and orchards occupied,
Hints how old owners went berserk or slack,
And as we enter into their mistake
And, edging nearer, re-enact their crime,

We see how many of us in trouble take
Pains with a staircase or a little rhyme.
All people in all ages have managed to pass the time.

The Romans, too. Country Trimalchios,
Turning local, wrangling with a Berber son,
Spat grapes on the mosaics of Volubilis,
Reinforced the old wall at Tarragon,
Staring at the sea, the past, that on and on
Lifts its enchanting and collective waves
And draws them back, dissolved, into its urn.
That hasn't changed much since the age of slaves.
Nothing changes. Nothing matters. Nothing saves.

But travelers wear down. After a while,
Overwhelmed by mountains, cathedrals, disorder, dirty underwear,
The nerves respond erratically, take coffee breaks, smile,
Burst into tears. Now and then, here and there,
Light forms, a moment streaks for the memory, air
Zithers with meaning, wings, wind suddenly rush
Into the mere market. Sooner or later, where
Did it do that, was it Meknès or Marrakesh,
One wonders, and one lets fall the brightness, the sweep, the hush.

Properly so. It is all medical, digestive,
Indicative of those interior travels –
Epic journeys of blood among the restive
Natives of nether regions, where reddened devils
Fight all night long to raise our sickening levels;
Passions of the lower organs; a flash-flooded stream –
No, a whirlwind – of loosening connections, lessening evils,
That blow away the cortex dream by dream.
Our wandering public life acts out this inner scheme.

Or both together do their ghastly dance.
My wife and I accord if music plays.
Within, without, the stately pairs advance.
Around us night's societies compose.
Tomorrow if all goes well, if it just goes
At all, we make for Conques or Vézelay
To see there, frozen in the sun and breeze,
How masters crafting their own crooked way
Carved in dense webs of stone *our* pilgrims' odyssey.

BEACH

Coming around the coast road at a crawl,
    Tense, sticky, yearning to be fresh and free,
We watch, divided, the gray highway curl
    A collar round the green and passive sea.
    Enchanted to a like passivity,
With tunics, towels, sandals, anti-bleach,
We join the naked persons on the peopled beach.

A comic theater, as it first appears,
    Where cloth is witty and elastic smug,
Where, as one enters (to quite muffled cheers),
    Broad daylight shows just what there is to hug.
    If some brown idiot laughs, it's best to shrug,
To claim, without a sigh or sulky word,
One's modest place among the physically absurd.

And, that achieved, one turns protected eyes
    To the performers in the bathing arts,
The girls with thighs like bellows, and the boys
    Whose public thews set off their private parts.
    How pleasing, as the heated pageant starts,
To scan the crooked energies of sex
From the unconscious kids to the regretful wrecks.

Treated by sun, what daydreams lead me on,
    What films in which desires are grown and granted!
Some thin delirium in the afternoon
        Lets life run where it will: no lie has counted,
        One cannot say what one has lost or hunted,
    Only that in this doze some fat and warm
Fish has pushed everything into its place and form.

And always near, the inattentive sea,
    That ventures no reflection or insight,
But keeps repeating – not at all to me –
        That message it has never got quite right,
        The sea that sniffles even in the night,
    Rounding the shoulders of its stones and creatures,
And unlike landscape lacks all visible fixed features.

The sea that . . . Till the cool, declining air
    And evening colors tinting the blue dome
Excite in us who swim or laze and stare
        The corresponding impulse to go home,
        To turn from the loose, finger-spreading foam
    Back to the closed fist and the heavy hand
Of the mute, firmly muscled, and yet yielding land.

With jokes, with mind – *Have we got all our things?* –
    We reappear upon the structured shore,
Resume for now the heat of horns and springs,
        The vigor days consume and nights restore,
        Though nothing stands quite as it stood before.
    Into the hills we drive tentatively,
And the dark parts for us like a collapsing sea.

ALARCÓN, 1966

Down below our hotel – a small castle, actually,
coaxed back only this year, for the delectation of
tourists, from its thirteenth-century suspicion and
malignity – down below, an enormous ravine
coils grassily around several strangled throats of rock
deeply eroded and slithers into the distance
like a scorched snake. Everywhere stone walls tell us we
are safe. Napping in our carved beds, confounding the day's
insolent heat, we grunt, open now to none but the
interior intrusion: What a relief to be above
the lower forms of anxiety! Some local boy may
steal our car, or the paperbacks we leave in it, but
murder is unlikely, the long disagreeable
struggle is done now, whose immodest aim was simply
to be physically secure. Of course, we regret it, we
hope for the bomb, make love to the stone-futile war and its
outcrop of courage. Still, when we emerge, eyes flooded,
from the dangerous picture-house and its grandiose wish
for all our lost violence, for the replenishment not
of castles but of victims, we know then how much more
than the light of day we have to face. Racks, turrets, gorge,
weapons on the wall – what can these do but function as
emblems of a different engagement, and of the myth
that it need not be fought, or has been won already?

Climbing up, in cooler, later air, round the round steps
as far as they go, to renovated ramparts, whence
to the glassed eye the true lie of the land is everywhere
open, we look down, love, order, faint trust edging our
unstilled doubt: it's all there, but so far down, so small, so . . .

Afraid, we touch the wall that touched our hand.
It turns into a person and we scream.

DAEDALUS IN SICILY

When we visited Heraclea Minoa, no one was there.
Our little car clung to the crooked road,
climbing its bumps and gullies to the sea.
Nobody met us, driving or walking, in or back.
No one was there, at the place, except for an old man
guarding the museum, who kept annotating the objects
and wanting to touch us, wanting us to join him in a beer.
We shook him off and strolled out to the theatre,
which is placed just at the headland, where the coast flinches
and you overlook both directions, as at a corner.

It was easy to imagine Daedalus there,
in his yellow kirtle, his shoulders gathered in exile,
the towns secure, all his great enemy's snares
raveled by art, easy to pick out his figure
toiling up to the watchtower behind the theatre,
still peering, every morning, to have word of Crete,
lost in the savagery of tangling thread, the local
flawed ceramic, chaos to the west, and down the blue
eastern channel the only chance of escape from
openness, avid air, compulsive touchers.

A Grecian Year

1. KAVALLA

November

Ferry-boats passing
blue clouds like an army of Romans advancing swiftly over Kavalla
and foraging eastward toward Xánthi and maybe toward Alexandroúpolis
the sun blinding above Thásos
the clouds that way swirled into cotton,
small gulls at rest, at swoop,
and the water below me, green near the shore, pounding the sand and
climbing
the long-suffering rocks.

A few miles north, at Philippi,
we saw just yesterday, this November, the field,
flat as a sea, where Cassius and Brutus, for sullen and contrary motives,
scrambled away their chance to be civil.
On that fixed plate of a plain,
good at eating up bodies,
neither the power principle nor the personal life comes clear.
Brutus is hacked beside Horace, who hawks his song,
and Cassius lives!

Where columns hold nothing up, and everyday streets
have lost their everyday clatter. Some stone stands
with disconnected conviction.
Confused ruins, comprising indistinct epochs,
I can make no sense of it.

Blue water, achingly bright,
sun on the pines and rocks,
the faltering remains of middle and ancient ages,
Byzantine, Roman, Ottoman, mine.

2. SEA MONSTER NEAR SALONICA

January

I

Walking this afternoon, late, on the pier,
in the off-season, out beyond the railings,
beyond the beach umbrellas and the heaps of shells

piled up by fiercer waves on violent days,
I found the sea, the air, uncommonly calm,
the city clear under clouds, and the mountains west and north

asserting lucid outlines, though the dark
was phasing down. A few ducks glided their rumps
over the purple surface. All the way down to the cape

there had been no one, the day just hung there, it was a dead place,
barely beating in the still season. Peering down
through water clear but evasive, I marveled at the litter –

tin cans, plastic sacks, cardboard cartons,
holders of force now released, relics, rubbish –
and at the life: seasnakes, starfish, dormant; and a sea monster, moving.

II

Not in Jacques Cousteau, not on film or behind glass,
not a contained menace but at large and live,
ourselves the only figures in the scene,

it on its side, I on mine (thank genes, or prehistory).
In front his mushroom bladder flapped pale brown
and pulled the bluish sponge that was the rest of him.

Not huge – perhaps a foot and a half in length
and about that wide in the bladder part – but shocking,
not built like any cousin, hence obscene,

he pulled under the pier first, brushed a grille,
then flailed slowly away in shallow water.
Lost? A precursor? I tried to give the thing a name,

envisioned it gorging, engorged, multiplied, taking over.
I looked around, it was winter, and no one to warn or wonder to,
as that image dimmed, came down to the damaged beach.

3. DELPHI

I

At Delphi it was damp.
Our approach from the north, past strong humps, had been fairly auspicious,
but once, leaning into a valley, the four of us watched
four black birds veer sharply down
to our left. Scarcely an hour later we
skidded scarily at a place where the road made a blind-angled turn
but came out of it, shaken and quiet.

Except for ourselves, the hotel at the top had been booked
by Americans in buses: *"Sure, the rain here is bad news,
but in Bronxville this year we've had mudslides."* Over drinks, past dinner,
our glance would slant down to the bay. At breakfast, in blue shorts,
an elderly jogger ran around the veranda –
some ancient herald, we joked,
whom no one would point out the path to the oracle.

II

What could I ask the god at this late date?
I have brought no votive offering.
I can only gaze down into the slate-blue harbor
where cruise ships pose their steel under still gray clouds
and try to imagine states of mind in which answers
struck into verse by resident poets working from the oral texts
of frantic Pythian priestesses could have solved anyone's problems.

Life, intense, layered, densely indifferent,
I have so long taken as enigma that I can't in conscience
entertain answers: landscape, seascape, soulscape
unfold daily, yearly, to all my credulous senses,
have meaning for me – color, composition, value –
but no transparent direction: the ships in the harbor
take others elsewhere in obedience to

purposes I can follow but cannot fathom,
the laws and orders by which such goings and comings –
to Delphi, Rome, Minneapolis –
are governed, by which I govern . . . whatever I govern.
But no fume swirls beneath the omphalos,
I heard no cry this morning from the oracular chasm,
to explain what this show is about.

III

One waits here, far above the sea, as minute by minute
the lights of Itéa go on, imagining evening
nine hundred thousand evenings ago
(you have to efface the hotels, the museums,
knickknacks have come a long way):
no cuts in the land, no quarries or slash roads,
nothing but crags, scrub, olive trees, fir, laurel, cypress,

as the traveler, through a dark world, guided by birds,
bent on his devious embassy,
picks his way up the green cleft, meter by meter,
the hairy lower approaches, past Athena's groinier precincts,
up toward the god's revelation hole, to submit,
with gifts dragged there by eight slaves, the throbbing, surrogate question:
Can I trust my queen? Has the war-moment come? Is it good for us
                                                        west of here?

Up the slope, hour after hour, into this snake-killer's country,
sinister, vested, severe, promising nothing but a word
uttered in trance and translated – but, heard, strong enough to
hurl any herald back down the ravine and onto the ship toward that
distant fat-fisted sponsor, waiting to ambush
his perfectly blameless barbarian second-in-sacking
or chop off his chief son's wrists.

IV

Suppose it was something like that. Or nothing like that.
Still trudging upward, glass in hand, late, to divine
that mantic scroll, the inward stream of the dead,
as if it could power our living. It has. It does.
To all interrogation reticent,
dead self, lapsed life, the ruined moment cry,
A god has danced here, I forget just why.

Back in the shops, in the town they hauled around the corner
to expose the oracle's nerves, fixed copyists glaze and paint
those pots and bronzes, replicas blank, uninflected,
like the tourists whose goods they become.
One Greek, on faint acquaintance, urges my wife to settle,
perhaps become a voice there, while I'm . . . wandering.
Our drachmas fetch an iron horse, and we

drive down as if we were changed, had composed ourselves, but
again,
on new terms, having learned on this height
from a holy mouth the conditions
under which new form affirms and strangles the old,
the harsh words screeching out the truth.
Oh yes, they're still packing 'em in at the Apollo –
damp, ominous, a joke, this talking hillside we've just now been up to.

4. RETURN

May

Dogs barking, shuddering music
from the all-night service station –
the price of warm nights.
Back, for two months in Greece,
from a Roman week
and a three-day Athenian coda,
to root in the sounds of dark
for my suite's order.

Stirred by the grave of Keats
and green-sinewed Poseidon –
AN ACTUAL EARTHQUAKE HERE
INTERRUPTED THIS NIGHTWORK –
I wonder about these untuned
liftings and shiftings,
feel giddy: *Is it still moving?*
Will this night arrest us?

As, under airport neons,
suspended between machines,
we waited, thoughtless,
a pool of blood today
by the baggage roller
(and leading in drops toward
the unfastidious taxis)
reminded us of our cycles.

One by one, the bolts
of the guilty bone-house buckle.
It's no good on fast hauls.
Conducted by fierce winds,
damp pain invades the thighs.
A cyst beneath my eye
requires to be cut.
I can't read long.

Soon, as the measures fly,
we'll be into the fourth movement
where more of the phrasing is obligatory
and the dogs cease to address
their howls at random.
Soon, by the tidal laws,
I'll be feeble as sand, as old
as Olga Rudge.

And one more shift
will have left its pavements behind –
tesseral archers, couching
lions and lachrymose conquerors,
blurred likenesses in briefs
(to a rakish string)
strolling away and waving
their love or money.

Driving to work,
Olympus in the rear-view mirror,
I keep going over my ever-
lengthening list of labors,
but the bloody rivers of Greece
and this heave-hoing
hurry the traffic along to
make room, man.

   Barely a moon later
   when the earth-bull grunted
and charged its unlucky dozens
breathless in rubble,
I still hadn't quite brought home this
bemused *seismòs*
but figure catastrophe's good for
one more strained stanza.

For everyone there's an end.
This salt democracy,
which is only one wave tall
from the point of view of our lives,
can heap great mounds of shells
on a vagrant beach
but in time will wash over
every field flower, driftwood

(*agrioloulòutha*),
the musical bones and the caco-
phonics who bruise them,
banked bakers and hourglass bodies,
peering into the dark
for the perfect loaf
or cruising the sands in search
of one's mislaid self.

Any palmist can read
the cracks in the storefronts.
The heaving goes on, we learn
to survive till we don't.
And if it was good to croak bass
in the only chorus so rich
it remembers others,
we shan't miss it.

5. EARTHQUAKE

Salonica, June 20

I

It will be easy to remember that night.
We thought *we* were entertaining.

Guests in the balcony box we'd wintered in!
To clinking glasses, the royal moon stepped on.

We watched her, over the hill where the sheep appear,
vaguely in the direction of the epicenter,

bowed to her tidal grace, then drove a troupe
to the seaside feedery down in the village.

There, under awnings, ordered – shrimp, fish, white wine,
shared talk, heads teetering closer, before high *"geiá sou,"*

occasion courtly but warm, waiters in voice,
the supporting weather tone-perfect, and I recall

our talking with mixed amusement and disquiet
of yesterday's mid-day quake when everything started

to quiver and rattle. We sat safe under the awning –
you could see people *knowing*, a clan scurried down from the

upper stage of the seahouse, and when it turned still
our friends rose up like waves to phone their children.

There's nothing much to do after an earthquake,
just see if the cast's still complete, check the props,

improvise patter, feel new powerlessness,
go on, this jolt, too, now our mask and make-up.

The dinner had been a success, quite unforgettable,
and no one was going to get drunk or stay on and on.

II

Only one quake is reported. For months friends will ask,
"Were you there for the earthquake?" and we, at a loss to conduct

those shocks, will keep on saying, "There were scores of quakes."
But talk, like the earth, shifts. A city's ups and downs

mean nothing much elsewhere. In and out of the news,
like local murders, private slopes of stress.

Even in Athens no one is much concerned
except for the dip in the national product.

III

One thing about earthquakes, I said, they're apolitical.
Yes, said my student Euripides, but the rich can get out.

IV

Lurking across the gulf night after night,
we drink scotch on the veranda, talk of friends, money, pride,
                                        the great disasters,

and furtively watch the city.
There are blank holes now in its bank of lights,

and we figure the flats are dark, waiting in dust
for the next move of the earth-shaker. The tenants,

with bundles and bread, have fled to the parks, or to wooded beaches,
and they camp there – here – day after day, waiting.

The days have been beautiful mostly, always sun,
clear sky, and the air so fresh it could be Arcadia.

Except, of course, for the tremors.
By day, at least some days, we all creep back,

needing the banks, the goods. It's an uneasy feeling
you have to have, with the still ungathered rubble

in the street of Ayia Sophias, the fallen chimney brickwork,
cracks in high walls, down church-walls, puddles of plate-glass,

men in despair on benches in bright morning.
Around the crumpled apartment house, spectators

watch the mechanized rubble-sorter sift
through tons of dust and an occasional corpse.

      . . . .

Our butcher's wife sits grim in her glass booth,
counts change, and with her eyes raised murmurs, *"Théos."*

We look up: the great flimsy roof of the market
spreads over us its uncertain guarantee.

6. XAIRETE!

end of June

Greece, we decide, packing up,
is glitter and arguing. Greece is

that past, what they "reared," what we climb,
the Hill of the Pnyx, Acro-Corinth,

photos we snap, eyes shut,
of these forerunners' frames. All

were different from us. All
blessed by the sea, by sunscape,

but within marked. Athens,
holding out hundreds of years

and guarding her pots and half-baked
hymns from uncivil Dorians,

has talked us, till now, into lasting.
Theater, history, thought:

our volume. They must, at Mycenae,
have gazed down past Argos to Nauplia

and held on, sailed off, meaning
power, meaning more chokers.

The poets buzzing at Athens
willed them a different dynasty,

a period – ours –
in which, we reflect, as we flick off

the lights, lock the door, leave the key,
what was shining was the bones.

OF LESBIA

51

That man there seems to me on the level of a god,
even, if it isn't a sin to say, higher than the gods,
who, sitting across from you, time and again
          watches and hears

you laughing lightly, a thing that drains poor me
of all my senses, for at the moment
when, Lesbia, *I've* looked on you I have no voice
          left in my throat

but my tongue goes dead, under my torpid joints
a fire licks out, my ears tingle with
their own noises, my eyes are hooded
          by a double night.

. . . .

Leisure doesn't agree with you, Catullus,
you enjoy leisure too much, you exult in it,
leisure has led to the ruin both of kings and
          prosperous cities.

After Sappho

86

To many Quintia is beautiful; to me her complexion is splendid,
    she's tall and stately: these details I concede.
That "beautiful," though, I wholly deny, for in so ample
    a body there's nothing lovely, no trace of brilliance.
Lesbia is beautiful, who to compose one perfect beauty
    has drawn from every woman her special grace.

83

When her husband's present, Lesbia says the most terrible things to me,
    which gives that fatuous man enormous pleasure.
Ass, do you see nothing? If oblivious of Us she were silent
    she'd be untouched but now by her snarling and railing
she not only acknowledges Us, but, what's much more telling, she's angry,
    which *proves* she's burning with passion and *has* to keep talking.

70

My woman says she'd be willing to marry no one
but me, not if Jupiter himself should woo her.

So she says

But what a woman says to a hot lover
has to be written in wind and running water.

8

Drooping Catullus, don't talk drivel,
let what you see has died be laid to rest.

You had your bright times once,
back then when you used to go where she presided,
that girl we loved as no one will ever be loved.

All those crazy things they did there then,
you willing, she not unwilling.
Yes, you had your bright times.
Now she says, No, no more; you too, drained, *you* say no,
don't chase her when she runs off, don't *suffer* any more,
but with a steady heart, hold on, be firm.

So long . . . girl. There, already Catullus is firm,
he'll not be needing you, not bother you:
see how you'll like not being bothered.
Bitch, how about that? What life will be left you then?
who will go near you? will anyone think you worth looking at?
whom will you love then, let it be said you belong to?
whom will you kiss? whose little lip will you bite?

But you, Catullus, stand firm, obdurate.

76

If a man can take pleasure in remembering
good he did once, when he thinks he's behaved decently,
broken no oath, made no bad use of gods
for some conspiracy against other men,
then many joys must loom in your lover's account, Catullus,
a long life's worth, from this merciless love.
For whatever good a person can say or do
for a person, you've said, you've done, only it's all
a dead loss, wasted on that ungiving girl.
Why, why do you this much longer torment yourself?
Why not tighten your will and make your way back
and, seeing the gods are against you, stop being miserable?

It's hard suddenly to put by a long love;
it's hard, but somehow – anyhow you can – do it!
This your one chance of health you must take hold of:
do it, whether you *can* do it or not.
O gods, if you do pity, or if ever you
brought help to someone death was creeping close to,
see how miserable I am, and if I've lived
purely, rid me of this plague, this cancer.
Torpor, O God, prowling through all my limbs,
has driven joy utterly from my heart.
I don't even ask now that she love me back,
or that she should – she *can't* – care to stay clean.
I want only to be well and to put off
this loathsome sickness. Gods, you *owe* me this.

11

Furius, Aurelius, friends who will stand by Catullus,
whether he journeys to the furthest Indies,
where the shore resounds long with the pounding
        wave of the dawn,

or to the Hyrcanians' land and the soft Arabs,
the Sagmen and the arrow-directing Parthians,
or where the nearer seven-engendering Nile
        bloodies the sea,

or whether he marches across the high Alps,
peering at monuments left by great Caesar,
to the Rhine of Gaul, the dreadful channel, and the
        remote British,

ready to risk all these things at once
or whatever the will of the gods enjoins on you,
convey to that girl of mine these few unkind
        words (will you?):

let her live and fare well with all the lovers,
three hundred at once, she keeps embraced,
caring for no one really, but breaking, time and again,
        the loins of them all,

and let her not look to have, as before, my love,
which by her fault fell, like a flower at the meadow's
edge, after it is touched by the
        plough going by.

58

Caelius, that Lesbia of ours, our Lesbia,
that Lesbia whom alone Catullus
more than himself and all his loved ones loved,

is now, at crossroads and in alleys,
peeling the proudpricked progeny of Remus.

10:   BACK FROM BITHYNIA

With nothing to do I let Varus
take me to check out his girlfriend,
little bitch (as I saw right away)
though not coarse really, not unattractive.

When we got there we fell into talk
of one thing and another, including
Bithynia, how I got on there
and just how much it put in my pocket.

I told her the truth: there was nothing
for natives, praetor, or staff
to let any palm come back well-greased,
much less if the praetor's a prick

who wouldn't spend shit on his staff.
"But surely," they say, "you must
at least have got men for a litter –
that's where they come from, isn't it?"

To get her to see me as fairly
flush, "Oh, it wasn't," I say,
"so bad that I couldn't pick up
eight well-built fellows for *that*."

(The truth is, I've no one here
or there who could lug on his back
the cracked foot of an old cheap bed.)
At which, as befits a slut,

she says, "Please, Catullus, lend me
yours for a while. I could use
a lift to Serapis." I told her,
"Wait a minute – oh, what I just told you

I had – I'd forgot – it's my friend
Cinna, that's Gaius, who owns them,
but his or mine, what does it matter?
I use them *as if* they were mine.

But you're really insipid and crude
not to know when a man's talking . . . loosely."

101 :   IN MEMORIAM FRATRIS

Having sailed past many peoples, many seas,
        I approach, brother, these grim obsequies
to give you up to the last rites of death
        and call on your speechless ashes, expecting no answer.
As fortune has robbed me of you, of yourself,
        poor brother undeservedly torn from me,
accept – all I can offer – these ceremonies
        come down from our fathers' time, sad gift to attend you:
tears of a brother have much watered them.
        And now forever, brother, hail and farewell.

Jiggling The Mirror

IMAGES

His oldest sister, Nellie, may have introduced Stephen to
the world of color and prepared him for an aesthetic
exploration of his environment.
— Jean Cazemajou, *Stephen Crane*

The face is missing, and no jaw was found with this
skull, but we have a jaw belonging to another individual
from the same deposit.
— L. S. B. Leakey, *Adam's Ancestors*

Safe, crumbling, dead . . . I give them back their life,
hold them there at the immense moment: Nellie
is leaning over Stephen, pointing at a color.
The color is in a book, she is preparing him
for an aesthetic exploration of his environment.

And now two stooping, globe-jawed, barefoot Tarzans
paw and circle, circle and paw. One bashes
the other's head in, which for him is a kind of
aesthetic exploration of the environment.
The bashee is visibly less exhilarated.

It takes only a word, only a breath,
to flood my theater with a bank of lights
and start the shadow-play. In Newark, in the Gorge,
Nellie, Stephen, Tarzan, do my dance.
I lean beyond them, bashed by every color.

POINT OF VIEW

This actually happened, it was real:
So poets in cool retrospection feel
Whenever after tantrums, trances, throes,
The cosmic and the personal compose.

> *I went to Italy, I searched the skies,*
> *I saw the Sibyl with my own two eyes.*
> *God breathed my name, light fled to the world's chinks,*
> *I sobbed and ran in terror from the Sphinx.*

The rest of us, helpless at what occurs,
Confronted by the life that ticks and stirs,
Nonplussed by persons, problems, bats, bears, burrs,
The real to which the poet's wand refers,

> More casual but equally elastic,
> Characterize all experience as *fantastic*.

LIES

No one tells lies like prophets.
They do it out of their great need
to be believed.

Experts lie: *you wouldn't understand,*
it's too complex,
take my word, I just know.

Mumbling vowels
about aggression,
persons in power dare not yield the truth.

The plain man,
jealous of all his learned itches,
hides from the light that could ease him.

Only the poet,
poor sick illusionist,
blows up lies into things as they are.

RIPOSTE

You still think poetry's the language of the soul?
     I wouldn't know, I'm sure, but who in this
scenario speaks to whom? Where do you find these folks
     equipped with spiritual wings and wordless whispers?
The ghosts I know use words, which for breaths light enough
     or shared enough have the effect of soul.
You and I leave an imprint looser mouths call love:
     to speak this stanza was a way of growing older.

HOW TO TALK TO A GHOST

For one thing, don't shout, no accredited ghost
is hard of hearing, speak in sentences
crisper than usual, but the phrasing should

be spare, natural, "rich, not gaudy." As to
meter, that's hard, better be guided by
your straining ear's due sense of the occasion.

If English is your language, speak in English.
Remember to tell something like the truth,
but delete all the data ghosts deplore

and vanish at first whiff of; try to avoid
abstraction, too, slut whose vulgarity
bores ghosts. Explain nothing but turn the minute

(you won't have more) to put grave rumpled questions
even ghosts take an interest in, though you
may scratch for years before you word one right.

Ghosts are to come, or not. If what you've roused
betrays no wish to shake you by the sheet,
hug silence, then devise a fitter sound.

IN THE BIG ROOM

The poet always slightly jiggles the mirror
(though he says not, though he swears this did happen),
and all of us know he does, we have to know

for his sake, as a child hiding with joy
knows that we know and don't know where he's hidden,
knows we agree to not know. There against

the oak dado the human face prepares
all the agreements that will see it through
warped life, and with the mirror makes its first

uneasy pact: left shall be right, and glass
grow space from nothing, coding what we know,
as if the mirror jiggled by itself.

DOWN THE LINE

This train, rumbling in place, about to go forward
forever, emitting strange gasps and hustled by
partly intelligent shouts, passengers squirting

up doors, down aisles, attending to baggage and children
and some at last, as the engine is almost ready
to draw them away, reflective now and at peace –

this train, I say, will not be stopped by a photo.
The soldier sprawled across three seats, the baby
bawling beyond consolation, the fat conductor

swaying but making progress forward backwards
as the coach car rattles over its crunch of distance –
we need these things to measure what they measure.

THE JOY OF POETRY

It's that, whatever image bubbles, we don't
have to explain. That's for the comment-persons,
which, in another life, we may be and in

all probability are. The bathtub gin
drained slowly. Knife after knife flew by his ear
while Corning waited, frozen. Neighbor boys

quarrel under the awning in the rain,
their innings disconnected, brown with baseball.
Do they tonight lug homeward still the trace

of forty, thirty, fifteen years' lost practice?
Only to catch, even at a distance, the diver
asleep in his dive or, high on the Southwest plain,

the frightfully wrong look of foundered cows,
by whose flame – yours, too? – I explain what it's been,
and is, to live, but not my explanation.

INSTRUCTION TO A POEM

Please take care of these feelings while I'm gone.
If anything happens to me, as it will,
let them not fall into the hands of linguists

to have their cup of syntax categorized,
their pools and fevers broken like a code.
You and I know, charged as we were to keep

their deepest structure in its plan of stone,
with well-disposed grimed bodies wedged in slits
to hold against any antagonist slighter than

sleep or time, what years of speech lie here,
what garbled measures poured, by some night's grace,
into this mold, which is not to be fingered

by an obsessed technician with bedpan skills,
sure to mistake its Tuscan doze for death.
If you must come before eyes, and you should,

may you be handled, like a skull in Kenya,
as if your exhumation gave a chance
to hold a breath, to enter someone's life.

SALVE

I

Whoever reads this poem,
if anyone reads this poem,

remember you know what I don't –
the footnotes will have confided it

or it will be common knowledge –
the year and name of my death,

how long and in what countries
I hung on after writing it

and whom, if anyone, I later
lost or came to be close to.

Your knowledge, my ignorance
shade a great gulf between us.

II

Whoever you are, if you even
glance at these words, or try

to make their glow your own
by more intense attention,

remember I know what you can't –
my space, the stairs, grounds, footpaths

I keep to, the famous faces
of all my unknown acquaintances,

the hairs on my hand, and the inner
faultscape of wrecks and blusters.

Your ignorance, my knowledge
shake the great bridge between us.

LEARNING PROCESS

These poems mean less to me year by year:
dry roots. And in the clearing hacked by time,
vanity, says my hardening soul, vanity,

no preacher. But this, this turn, like twisting streets
unlooked for, suddenly come on, has its own grave
force, its white page. What widening it is

to dip the child's pen, Miss Lizzie's eye closed,
into the well of experience one has casually
also become, to scrawl, behind the hour,

its handless, hard, and harrowing design.
The engraving done, this dawn, time for the house
to cry awake: messages, barricades, refreshments, money.

REMEMBERING

Whatever happens, let it pass – it must!
– then quietly, as if it had to help,
alter its speech, its purposes. Not lies:

call it remembering, the image made
radiant with our truths. Yesterday's lunch,
the chase last summer in the park, some quarrel

half become history, what you said, I did
– none of it (need it matter?) as it was:
the day we drove Alex to Avignon

finding in his false courtliness a key
to us, France, fall, the Palace of the Popes.
All the way back his talk gored instances.

REJECTION SLIP

Another rejection: "*We hate to do this to you,*
but we get so goddamn much mail. Sorry. We really
like you." Better at least than the insolent note

I got last year from a leading acronym:
"*A deal too talky for us.*" The very first time
when, at a friend's urging, I sent out poems

I received a courteous, gentle note from John Crowe
Ransom and since have built a unique collection
(now long dismantled) of no-slips, almosts, of-course-nots

(one said, "*You must be kidding!*") and "*Try us next decade*
when our backlog has unjammed." Bill Stafford claims
to think rejections are just the good editor's way

of saving him from his less fine self, which is
okay if you're Stafford, sure that your poems won't be
turned down lightly, but what if you're talky, and me?

· · · · · · ·

What if you are? The only editor I know
personally died yesterday morning. When I saw him last,
he was saying, "*Help me, help me,*" and I said, "*I will, I will.*"

MOTTO FOR A MIDDLE-AGED POET

A stanza a day
Keeps despair away.

MEETING A YOUNG POET

We chat in someone's kitchen of poetry –
his, mine, anyone's. He has been learning this year,
in spite of changes, burdens, to keep on.

Is he deluded? He must think I am:
"This ancient party still creeping through kitchens
without a volume – " But I'm a voice he knows

he needs, at least tonight, to speak of our
vocation. He must have faint hope that my slapdash
works will last out the century, and why should his

lyrical cheek persuade me he has talent?
Jabber and a smell of gas aside, we know
the same unquiet service has required us.

ON TRANSLATING CATULLUS

It's strange to think of Catullus as having my feelings
without my background. He'd hardly read anything,
not a single line of the Romantic poets or Shakespeare,

didn't even know English, which is almost a prerequisite
for a poet whose subject is me. Somehow he managed,
in spite of these classical failings, to blunder into

our song. Funny, unhappy, suspicious, accusing,
collecting all the arguments against pain
in tones that change color when you go near them,

he resisted, resisted, and he displayed himself
refusing to know how powerless he was,
how will fails, how passion sometimes is

almost entirely agony. A thousand thanks,
model, Catullus, and lover, for bitter words,
which in a tough season I turned into these.

FOR BERRYMAN, 1972

Touch words together many million times
(your nature), then once all at once go speechless,
bed rock, rock bottom, 'stead of bottomed girls.
Grieving for ruined hamlets, fall like a bomb
that flares grief but kills no one, reaches
in fragments strangers, worlds.

Kills no one *else*. But though
the music doesn't quit, the great jazz
jubilation piano's not there this week
to invent or improvise.
The piano is closed. Except maybe Auden, no
one still tripping keys can touch its technique.

For a time now talk turns leaden.
Maybe he found a craftsman's way to stop it,
stop words, stop writing, maybe
living that tellingly long just deadens:
words left but no transitions, just light to cap it
by leaning forward, candy from a baby.

FOR W.H. AUDEN, FEBRUARY 21, 1989

You looked a hundred at least in your last few
years, but if you had lived, old Sly Boots, just till
this a.m., you'd only have rung the year-scale
        at eighty-two.

Country's of no account, though, after the cold's
in place. Still, here in brisk Minnesota (your
kind of frostscape), let this day in syllabics
        be scored Auden's.

PORTRAIT OF CREELEY

the one-
eyed poet beats
time to
his lines, jerk-
ing his
finger and
voice to the one-
upbeat

in his mild
throat care-
less words get
long
lost, his
hesi-
tations like
little anx-
ie-
ties dra
g us into ear-
shot

in there
small
bells must
always be
bonging like crazy

SMALL DARK POET READING

My lot is a happy one. Here is a poem.

My wife and I are very close. Here is a poem.

A young lady whose name I forget asked for a poem. Here it is.

Here is a poem about my marvellous kids.

RANDY POET

I

Earlier, but not on time,
he shows in a suit, his hair
brushed wild, eyes searching the slanting

hall for applause, as he combs
his goods and explains each item's
signaling devices, a seasoned

performer, ready with riveting
gaze and his thin, crowded
volume of phrases.

II

Later, after the scheduled
punch-bowl, chit-chat blast,
almost on call, he'll give,

grateful for her expected
homeness and warmth, a whisper
of his more secret syntax

sliding into her love-book,
prompt and blurred as a postman,
to forge his signature.

ICING

The hard poets, opaque, brilliant, stretching
like ice for miles, dread glitter, till, as phrase
glides into phrase unblinding strangely, we see,

just see, we begin to see, and the hard lake,
section by section uncaking, turns blue, turns mirror –

till the next numbing season freeze it over.

THE POET AS STAND-UP COMEDIAN

Taking a clothesline from his rucksack, the poet slowly unwinds it,
      coils it straight up in the air, snaps it into a curtain,
whips two or three members of the audience with it, then murmurs quizzically,
      "Lately I've been trying to work with the long line."

POETRY AS A PLASTIC ART

This poet is like a man who goes on making
the same exquisite jars, year after year,
each combining the shades and the light and the shapes,
and the detail of the shapes, in slightly differing
jars.
      One feels, one of these beautiful things
should be in every city along the earth.
But the mind is too small a room, they hide each other.
Worse, nobody even has an impulse to break them.

POEM AND FILM

for Neil Isaacs

Yes, but a poem can never effect that total
absorption, that attention and a half, of a film.
Anything may distract, a doorbell, some stray
voice, an alien thought, flare of remorse

may edge the phrase from vision and the eyes collect
whole days or years beyond it, later resume
lost thread – whereas in the strong movie nothing
from one's actual life is actual, one witnesses, witnesses

terrible murder, dreams in company
that woman's anguish, that child's course of guilt,
scene after scene quickens one's cry for life,
years drift back, images, smoke, even the decor

of Robert Lowell's poems can't begin to touch it,
some soul's brought to light there. Then what are poems good for,
their shadows of images, voice-traces, stains,
their memories of echoes of reflections?

*　*　*　*

Dim, dim – yet my lips love to say their words
patterned and indeterminate, like life,
yes, more like life, slow life, slow troubled life,
that huge slow-seething frame that holds me, holds . . .

BREATHING SPACE

Now that I've written
my undoubted masterpieces
on which no day's dust
will likely settle,

it is time for exhaustion and weaning
and the dog-eared volume
of little talk, money,
reviewing my golf game, my junk pile,

before my shut-in,
cranky, obsessed author
claims my clutter again
for his art-object.

EPITAPH

He loved his wife, a dog, and poetry.
Sprinkle his ashes ceremoniously.
Thanks, friends who've shared this golden hitch with me.

Epilogue: DERBY DAY, 1994

For Tekla Alida Ingeborg Anderson Wright

(b. May 7, 1894)

Our hats, our Hertz, off to you this day, clearly
a runaway winner, Mother, down any stretch.

I

Six years ago I saw it first, the framed
photo of you at sixteen, facing forward,
ready for any century or challenge,
your fingers at the hem of your 1910 skirt,
the angle of your head defiant – saw it
over your shoulder as you played at bridge.
Nearer, yourself at ninety-four, less assured,
puzzling your hand – *Is that the ten of spades?* –
still straightening the dummy: the same gaze
after eighty years of deep finessing,
a time-lapse layered in the family room.

That string of Swedish names, capped by your father's
patronymic, steered your growing up
in a hardworking Brooklyn neighborhood,
your lifelong learning founded at Girls' High.
You and your best friend there still correspond,
your hand as steady now as when, at fifty,
you wrote me via V-mail. Sometimes, in play,
proud of possession, you sign your letters *"Me."*

Quickness and shorthand earned you office jobs,
mainly with lawyers for the Guggenheims,
picking up Spanish, stories, background, skills.
You met our father (so the story goes)
on a summer evening's hay-ride in the Catskills,
tickled the back of his neck with a straw, and so

scratched an acquaintance – all our current lives
the consequence of that casual flirtation.
You know what followed: war, Dad's time in France,
marriage, a home on hilly Staten Island,
Depression troubles, money problems (Life!).
I've stored stressed images of both your youths:
Dad trying out new ways to stay afloat,
insurance, bank work, miniature golf,
before the long, steady career with Swift;
you holding house together, toiling over
washtub, coal bin, icebox, ironing board;
while we survived the childhood illnesses,
enjoyed the challenge of the one-room school,
kids' baseball on the vacant lot next door,
sleds in snow-time, croquet and crabs on the Manasquan,
hardly aware at all of your anxieties,
yet somehow learning how to craft our own.

 Mother, you gave us all our point of view,
our place to stand, our being in the world,
watched over us with interest and affection,
not always patient, never negligent,
angry at moments, sometimes hurt to tears.
You taught us love – and how to tie a shoelace.
You read a lot, as much as you could manage,
had strong opinions, mostly about conduct,
were curious, verbal, shy but forceful, earnest
often but willing, too, to be amused,
enjoying Sunday drives, vacation scenes,
strolls down the boardwalk, radio's Ellery Queen,
troweling in your garden, shooing birds,
games, puzzles, cards, light jokes, and plays on words.
Once you won a drawing at the local movie house.
When you waltzed home that night, we all woke up
to help you celebrate your luck, as life,
beaming and friendly, gave you one good break,
auguring more to come. Earlier, when
a late and listless appendectomy

almost destroyed me, it was you who kept
a diary of my dangerous days and nights.
The look of your concern still touches me.

　　　After some twenty years on Staten Island –
strange isle, part city annex, part small towns,
our scenic dump, where sixty years have worked
no change in most of our familiar streets,
but a rude Bridge transmuted all the rest,
borough detached, now fixing to secede –
you took the move up-city in your stride.
In some ways it was simpler: an apartment,
no house, to manage, but no garden either,
uptown, live Broadway, the eleventh floor,
between a great magician and a jeweler.
In that smart, multi-cultured neighborhood,
where pigeons and sopranos exercised,
their tones and turds sprinkling the air we breathed,
our elevator, manned and manual, set us
down near the rumbling underworld, to which
heroic statues guarded the descent.
High above, in your sky-bright cave, in view
of the library pediment across which names
HORACE TACITUS ST. AUGUSTINE ST. THOMAS AQUINAS DANTE
witnessed for mind each morning, you could watch
(as if in shadow on another wall)
your own brood growing, till the new war drew
two sons in turn, took Norma to Tacoma,
then shipped them all back briefly. Post-War, rents
froze, and your wayward young skipped west and south,
drifted from coast to coast, from time to time
settling in all the regions. Still at home
in confident Manhattan, fifties folk,
you and Dad throve on television, Scrabble,
the N.Y.A.C. and a worldly life,
not rich but most agreeable, spiced with concern
about "the children," till they found their form
and flourished modestly. You see them now,

retired, gathered here to cheer you on
as you begin your second century.

II

Last year, on your ninety-ninth, steering our Hertz
through Louisville's intricate net of intersecting
avenues, turnoffs, detours, we asked you whether
the route we were risking was right. You weren't sure.
You'd been driven it scores of times, but it wasn't where you
had spent your major life: here wasn't home.
"If I'd known I was going to live this long," you told us,
"I'd have paid more attention."

That second century starts its count today.
No guarantees on this one, but good genes
can do a lot. Some proof of it is here:
your kids have made it this far down the track,
nearing or numbering seventy. Some of theirs
have kept your string alive, and Kevin, Danny,
Alex are in the cheering stands today.
"Stay with us," as the news announcers plead,
"There's more to come." Eyes young as yours or ours
won't be around to clock them down the years,
but, interested, still curious, still strong-hearted,
with so much of the what's-to-come uncharted,
you're here to take a look at what you started.

Another six years and you will have lived
in three distinctive centuries – why not,
as long as you've an eye for reading and
a big hug for each great-grandchild, their small
fingers uncertain how to seize your age.
One of them, say, might live as long as you,
last till the twenty-second century,
and wonder at the changes in his life
that will have registered in every cell
at information-superhighway speed.
That would be something fabulous to see;

I hardly need say, none of us will see it.
We'll settle for a less protracted term –
eighty or so, or maybe ninety-two,
time enough for all we still wish to do:
some travel, music, leisure, love, and tennis,
and, neutralizing darker thoughts of menace,
more Derby weekends celebrating you.

FIFTEEN MONTHS LATER

Death, intolerant of laggards,
found you off guard, took advantage,
ambushed you in your apartment,
set you flailing, frightened, quickly
                breathless, pulseless.

In a week, by will and magic,
you were home again, near normal,
with the universal stricture
non-compliant for the moment.
                For the moment.

Tekla died May 2, 1997.

George T. Wright was born on Staten Island in December 1925, attended Columbia College, and served in the U.S. Army in 1944-46. He has taught at the Universities of California (where he earned his Ph.D.), Kentucky, Tennessee, and Minnesota, and as a Fulbright Lecturer, at Aix-Marseille and Thessaloniki. After twenty-five years at Minnesota, he retired as Emeritus Regents' Professor and now lives in Tucson, Arizona, with his wife of forty-three years. His scholarly writings include "The Lyric Present: Simple Present Verbs in English Poems" (1974), "Hendiadys and *Hamlet*" (1981), and *Shakespeare's Metrical Art* (1988).